In Fear of Each Other

The Dangerous Offender Project

JUSTICE

John P. Conrad and Simon Dinitz
Project Co-Directors
The Academy for Contemporary Problems

In Fear of Each Other

Studies of Dangerousness in America

John P. Conrad
Simon Dinitz
The Academy for Contemporary
Problems

Lexington Books

D.C. Heath and Company
Lexington, Massachusetts
Toronto

Cover: Cuneiform characters for the word *Justice*, the emblem of the Dangerous Offender Project.

Library of Congress Cataloging in Publication Data

Main entry under title:
   In fear of each other.

   1. Crime and criminals—United States—Addresses, essays, lectures.
2. Insane, Criminal and dangerous—United States—Addresses, essays, lectures. 3. Violence—United States—Addresses, essays, lectures. 4. Corrections—United States—Addresses, essays, lectures. I. Conrad, John Phillips, 1913- II. Dinitz, Simon.
HV6791.I52   364.3   77-286
ISBN 0-669-01478-8

Published simultaneously in Canada.

Printed in the United States of America.

International Standard Book Number: 0-669-01478-8

Library of Congress Catalog Card Number: 77-286

To our secretary
Sherry Flannery
whose endurance, tact, and good humor
made this book possible

Contents

Preface

The concept of dangerousness is neither a new nor a particularly specific construction. Like so many other pseudodiagnostic categories, it has crept into the language of the law, the clinical professions, the law enforcement community, and into the media and lay terminology. A local broadcaster, known for his penchant for hyperbole, consistently referred to dangerous criminals as "vermin who crawl in the night." This memorable, if overblown, phrase encapsulates the denotative quality of the term "dangerousness": an amorphous admixture of madness and badness resulting in injury, suffering, harm, and fear to innocent victims and to that fragile social network known as society. In its popular rendition, dangerousness implies a quality, a set of attributes, and a character structure and personality that are evil, unsocialized, unpredictable, and beyond remedy. The senseless and brutal robber who pistol whips his victim qualifies; so does the child molester, the chicken hawk who kills his young boy pickups; the rapist, the uncontrollably enraged predator, the brutal assaultist, and the too many other bizarre and not so bizarre violent criminal offenders who are often spread across the front pages of our newspapers.

Dangerousness, whatever it is, is not a legal concept although it is embodied in a variety of criminal statutes such as habitual criminal offender laws, sex psychopath statutes, and the insanity, incompetence and other codes. Dangerousness is also not a psychiatric-psychological term yet it permeates and indeed is central in nearly all clinical decision-making concerning violent inmates—from the initial determination of the need for psychiatric observation to the final decision about return to the community. Dangerousness is not a statistical concept, either. Still, nearly all predictive instruments are predicated on the desire, if not the ability, to forecast future violent behavior and recidivism.

No discipline can now lay claim to great expertise about the identification, treatment, and control of dangerousness. The focus on dangerousness is a major constraint on the functioning of the criminal justice system at all levels. The public increasingly demands that the streets be swept clean of dangerous persons even if it means abrogating due process guarantees.

In this climate of what Kierkegaard, in another context, called "fear and trembling," many dead issues in criminology have been resurrected: punishment, deterrence, justice, career criminals, and criminal careers. Especially pronounced is the cyclical return of interest in the hoary issue of dangerousness.

In 1975 the coeditors of this volume undertook a comprehensive investigation of several important segments of the problem of the identification, treatment, and control of the dangerous offender. We did so for some very practical reasons. We believed then as we do now that reforms in the correctional, judicial, and enforcement fields will not come unless the public fear about the dangerous offender can be allayed. Communities will continue to resist locally based facilities as long as they remain in mortal fear of violent ex-offenders or diverted delinquents as neighbors. No amount of persuasion is likely to alter this thinking. The gains of the last few decades in deinstitutional-ization, due process, and decriminalization have already lost much of their appeal to a fearful electorate.

Another reason for embarking on this dangerous offender study was the involvement of the Academy for Contemporary Problems' Crime and Justice Center in producing a new Declaration of Principles concerning the treatment of offenders. *Towards a New Corrections Policy: Two Declarations of Principles* was both a commemorative and an appeal to conscience and action. It was a commemorative in that in 1870 the initial principles were enunciated by some crusty old wardens and dedicated reformers. This 1870 meeting also marked the origin of what is now the American Correctional Association. In confronting the issue of prison reform and the guidelines for sentencing, advocacy, and imprisonment, the question of dangerousness could not be cast aside as irrelevant. The declaration enunciates the first maxim for corrections: *Let the sentence be administered in such a way as to increase the probability of the offender's reconciliation with society when his restraint is complete.* In discuss-ing sentencing practice, however, the first general principle is: *Incarceration should be restricted to certain offenders whose recorded criminal behavior indicates that the protection of society cannot be afforded in any other way, or where surveillance in the community has been without effect . . . .*

The Lilly Endowment sponsored the Dangerous Offender Project that initiated research in the following areas:

1. the concept of dangerousness in the legal codes
2. a history of dangerousness with special emphasis on the changing concep-tions of the concept, and altered views of etiology and treatment
3. the neurobiology of violence: past, present, and future paradigms and practices from a biomedical perspective
4. the dangerous adult offender: twenty-five years of violent offenders arrested by the police in Columbus, Ohio
5. the prosecution and incapacitation of the dangerous criminal
6. a multistate study of the dangerous offender in prison: predators and victims behind the walls
7. the dangerous juvenile delinquent: five birth cohorts of violent offenders
8. the prediction of dangerousness
9. ethical issues in the identification, management, and control of the violent offender

The first three investigations are complete as of July 1977. Two volumes have been produced, and the first—about dangerousness and the legal statutes—

has been published by Lexington Books. The historical treatise is also complete. This book is an overview, in article form, of some of the other major initiatives of the Dangerous Offender Project; it is designed to set the tone of the overall endeavor. With but one exception, it does not present the results of our painstaking empirical research on the onset, progression, and extinction of adult violent careers nor of their juvenile counterparts. We have impressive data on these matters, and others, on some 1600 adults and five birth cohorts of juveniles, 1138 in all, and of these 811 who have reached eighteen years of age and legal adulthood. Nor are we presenting our data on the prosecution of 1217 consecutive cases in a typical Middle Western county. The last of the four major empirical studies—the solitary confinement investigation—is discussed in general rather in terms of specific data that will be available later and separately.

The first chapter in this volume concerns Stephen Nash, a bumbling but pleasant Soledad inmate, who was apparently harmless within the limits of his abilities. Released to parole, Nash murdered seventeen skid row derelicts without seeming cause or rationale. Cheerful as ever, Stephen Nash, the "nondangerous" buffoon, was executed for his crimes without leaving clues about his motive. Could this brutality have been averted? Who is to blame? What could have been done to prevent it?

George Clancy, the boy nobody wanted (not his parents, foster parents, the schools, the juvenile court, the juvenile correctional system, his city, and not even the state in which he was born) was by age fourteen or shortly thereafter a media event. To the press, he was a "monster" who committed a series of violent and vicious crimes combining robbery, sexual depredations, and grievous bodily harm. His sorry saga tells us much about how a young man grows up violent. It tells us even more about the inadequacies of the juvenile justice system. George Clancy's acts were bizarre indeed. Yet his is neither a unique pattern nor the most outrageous history among the "residents" of a maximum security juvenile training school. The chapter is included to highlight our current inadequacy in identifying, preventing, or even managing the George Clancys of the system.

The third chapter reviews the literature on the psychopathic/sociopathic/ antisocial personality in relation to dangerousness, on the one hand, and chronically antisocial behavior on the other. The essence of an experimental treatment program is briefly described.

At another level, the current paradigms concerning the biological substrates of violent behavior are carefully reviewed. The author suggests that we may be entering a period in which our understanding of the biomedical aspects of behavior is qualitatively different than at any time in the past. We stand at the brink of major breakthroughs at this level. The issue may no longer be the inadequacy of our understanding but the social control of our knowledge. Professor Goldman is sensitive and concerned about the intrusive biomedical interventions—pharmacological, psychosurgical—recommended and used with humans. While detailing a new nonintrusive line of intervention (polypeptides) that alter the internal environment, he cautions against the tendency to reduce social problems to personal pathologies.

The next selection is based on a participant-observer study of professional decision-making in a hospital for the criminally insane. Based on a federal court order, twelve three-member teams of outside experts were empaneled to evaluate all residents to be released, transferred to a civilian mental hospital, or assigned to continued safekeeping in Ohio's Lima State Hospital for the Criminally Insane. The decision was predicated on the potential dangerousness of the prisoner-patient. The definition(s) of dangerousness, their specific application in individual cases, and the team's negotiations in arriving at a conclusion make a fascinating chronicle of the clinical professions in the forensic field.

A number of writers have argued that rehabilitation-reform is an impossible dream; the public would be better served by an honest policy of incapacitation. The authors examine the effectiveness of this proposed remedy, postulating a very stiff penalty. For violent crimes, the prevention rate of this fixed sentence is estimated to be in the 4-percent range; for crimes cleared and persons charged, the rate is in the 18-percent bracket. In neither case is incapacitation as a sentencing goal seen to be an effective option.

The next-to-last chapter presents an overview of solitary confinement and protective custody practices and problems in the traditional fortress prison. Since 1972 the atmosphere of the prison has changed markedly. Ethnic, racial, and religious antagonisms from the outside have been brought within the walls. Violence has taken on a group flavor. While individual predators still stalk the yard, the gangs—Neo-Nazis, Nuestra Familia, Mexican Mafia, Conservative Vice Lords, the Bikers—have usurped much of the power once exercised by the now cowed administrators. This chapter describes these changes and questions the conventional wisdom of the inmate culture theme that focused our thinking from Donald Clemmer's pioneering work to the present.

The last chapter deals with the very thorny ethical issues raised by the prevention and treatment of dangerousness. Although geared to correctional practice, much the same issues are raised in the biomedical and psychiatric assessment of dangerousness articles. These crucial issues speak to the most democratic and human concerns—the tension between conflicting individual rights (to treatment, to be left alone) and the right of a collectivity to protect its members. Both rights are fundamental, and each may infringe on the other.

John P. Conrad
Simon Dinitz

In Fear of Each Other

1

What Happened to Stephen Nash? The Important Questions About Dangerousness

John P. Conrad

I spent the better part of 1954 as a middle manager at Soledad State Prison, which was later redesignated, without any other perceptible change, as the Correctional Training Facility (reflecting the then prevailing belief in California that emphasis on training prisoners would produce better effects than an emphasis on incarceration). Still later, Soledad was to achieve a notoriety equalling that of San Quentin, its sister prison, as the place where George Jackson wrote *Soledad Brother*,[1] and as the site of murderous confrontations between black inmates and white guards. All that was still to come while I was the prison's Classification and Parole Representative, but even then Soledad was a restless place. Prisoners who were transferred there expected that conditions would be better than in the other California "correctional facilities." Unfortunately, they found the same restrictions and humiliations, and their disappointment was expressed in frequent disciplinary infractions and occasional collective disturbances.

My responsibilities during that year consisted of liaison with the Adult Authority (as Californians then designated their parole board for reasons lost to history), the classification of prisoners, and the management of the processes that transformed prisoners into parolees. Sooner or later I would have an encounter with each of the 1400 men confined at Soledad. For an aspiring criminologist, it was a satisfying opportunity to meet and come to know a wide variety of interesting criminals.

One of them whose memory haunts me was Stephen Nash, a bony, acne-scarred, and toothless young man who was the prison buffoon. Always in minor trouble, never harming anyone, he was usually kept in our segregation unit. We thought he lacked the defenses that would protect him in the daily rough and tumble of prison life. He had a long record of minor rule violations; a typical one was the destruction of state property. One afternoon he was listening to the World Series, and the shortstop of the Yankees, his favorite team, committed a crucial error. He tore off his earphones and stamped on them. The Disciplinary Committee, of which I was a member, laughed indulgently and he laughed ruefully. We did what we had to do, and he cheerfully accepted another stretch in isolation.

Eventually Nash was released from Soledad, with no parole because he had served his complete ten-year maximum sentence. But it was not long before he was in the headlines, and our indulgent chuckles were silenced in appalled

1

dismay. Nash had been arrested and charged with seventeen murders of skid row derelicts, mostly by strangling. He cheerfully admitted all of them and had no comprehensible explanation for his ferocity. He was tried, convicted, and sentenced to the gas chamber, an end that he seems to have accepted just as cheerfully as in years gone by he had taken his medicine in the isolation wing at Soledad. While on the San Quentin condemned row he infuriated the other residents by reciting in gory detail the particulars of those seventeen strangulations.

At Soledad, Nash served an indeterminate sentence of one to ten years for grand larceny. His release at the maximum end of that sentence was required by law. No correctional decision-maker could be reproached for an error in judgment. The public had been protected for a full decade because Nash had never been able to put together the six months of "clean conduct" required at that time for consideration for parole. I do not have the slightest doubt that if he had managed those six months of clean conduct he would have been released many years earlier with no apprehension that anyone would be imperiled. The members of the Adult Authority were reasonable. To hold the likes of Steve Nash, that sadly amiable clown, in an expensive prison cell for a grand larceny that was not really grand—a till-tapping amounting to around $100—made no sense. But rules were rules, and in this case they protected society better than we knew.

A few weeks after his release, Nash was arrested for indecent exposure. A psychiatrist interviewed him, found no hint of significant disturbance, and recommended his return to his apparently aimless wandering. The next arrest was for those seventeen homicides. A renowned forensic psychiatrist, who examined him with appropriate care and thoroughness, elicited an account of a bleak childhood in children's institutions and foster homes, the shuffled relocations of the unloved and unwanted. The nation's prisons and mental hospitals contain hundreds of men and women with similar histories, but few could match Stephen Nash in hidden malignancy. The psychiatrist frankly confessed his inability to discover anything unusual about him to account for his murderous career.

Nash was a unit in the murder statistics of that mid-fifties year. He fits into a category in some taxonomy of violent crime. He was also a flesh-and-blood human being. He was not an abstraction, nor was he a two-dimensional character for an illustrative anecdote. He was perhaps the most dangerous man I have ever known. He was also a part of that endless stream of people in chambray and denim who flow through the country's prisons year after year, so easy to count, so hard to know. The memory of Steve Nash will serve well as a symbol of the most frustrating dilemma in working toward prison reform.

The Dangerous City

The modern prison originated in the early nineteenth century, and ever since then it has been the object of reform attempts. Ideals have flickered out in a coercive system in which ideals cannot flourish. Some abuses have been abolished, but the miserable realities persist. The nature of the prison requires a closed community that is incompatible with the open society. Because all measures tried have failed to modify the inherent degradation, hostility, and violence, reformers in the last ten years have proposed the "deinstitutional-ization" of criminal justice—in short, the elimination of the prison as an instrument of social control. A whole literature of prison abolition has been written, and a zealous movement is under way to prevent, by a policy of moratorium, the building of more prisons.[2] Concerned with the application of knowledge to the resolution of social dilemmas, the Academy for Contemporary Problems sponsored a prolonged discourse of prison administrators and criminol-ogists to discover the principles by which a correctional system could be made compatible with a democracy committed to fairness and decency.[3]

The punishment of property offenders by measures short of incarceration appeared feasible and desirable to all. But deinstitutionalization could go no further: Along with nearly all contemporary critics of the criminal justice system, the group agreed that the dangerous offender had to be confined for the public's protection. Sentences for the violent offender had to be served in prison, though there was agreement that for most of this class shorter terms might be imposed. Each participant had a symbolic figure in mind—mine was Steve Nash—but no one was ready with a definition of dangerousness. Clearly we needed studies of the nature of dangerousness, its incidence, the laws governing it, and the possibilities for remedies and treatment. Fortunately, means for the Dangerous Offender Project became available to the academy.

The reality of the problem is indisputable. Steve Nash was dangerous and proved it too late for anyone to intervene. But had the clinicians perceived his true potentiality during those years at Soledad, what should they have done? What could be done in a similar case, twenty years later? Medical, ethical, and legal issues abound, but without reasoned resolution. The emotional response to Nash was one of extreme retaliation: extermination after all his victims were dead. Knowledge and understanding should improve society's response to the danger-ous few and perhaps will reduce the number whose dangerousness is fatal to others.

Public pronouncements about crime in the streets suggest that violent people present new perils to the inhabitants of American cities. Too many Americans live in continuous fear of roving muggers and brutish rapists, and FBI statistics justify their fears. But urban violence is nothing new. Wise house-holders who were fortunate enough to live in Florence during the age of Michelangelo and Galileo kept off the streets at night; the memoirs of Benvenuto Cellini vividly recount the hazards encountered by the unarmed and unwary. The ferocity of the English criminal law in the eighteenth century, so obviously benighted to our eyes, was inspired by the sturdy rogues and vagabonds who mugged honest London burghers, raped their wives, and sometimes controlled a great deal of the countryside. In this country, the dark streets and alleys of nineteenth-century Boston, New York, and Chicago were just as unhealthy for ordinary citizens after daylight as they have been in recent years.

Cities have always been dangerous. Some, like Edward Banfield in *The Unheavenly City*,[4] argue that efforts to make them safe are wasted. The transformation of the American city into Utopia is beyond anyone's power, but there is no excuse from effort to reduce the intolerable burden of violence that citizens now endure. Toward this end, criminologists can at least order existing knowledge and make some modest interpretations of experience.

The perspective of the recent past accounts for some of the civic discontent. What is known of the crime and turbulence of American cities in the nineteenth century comes from historical rather than statistical evidence. FBI data extend back to the 1930s, but the figures are dismaying. From a relatively comfortable level of criminality as recently as the mid-sixties, the situation has deteriorated dramatically. In 1960, for example, the robbery rate in Columbus, where the Dangerous Offender Project is based, was 79.1 per 100,000. This rate descended to 54.4 in 1962. It rose steadily and almost perpendicularly to its 1975 level of 267.0 per 100,000. The rate for the same crime in Cleveland moved even more spectacularly, from 81.7 in 1960 to 429.5 in 1975. A few cities in the United States have not experienced this vertiginous sloping of the violent crime rate. An example is Tulsa, remarkable because its robbery rate has risen from 62.1 in 1960 to the still modest level of 113.8 in 1975.

Criminologists have engaged in critiques of the FBI's statistical methods for many years. The lack of adjustment of rates to intercensus changes in the composition and size of the general population is a conspicuous defect; so is the lack of any routine procedure for an audit of reports transmitted from the police departments of the nation to the central collecting office. But a trebling of the robbery rate in my city, a quintupling of the rate in the neighboring city of Cleveland, and even more disturbing contrasts in other cities cannot be explained away by reference to more efficient recording or self-interested manipulations of the statistics. If American streets are to become safer, those who are responsible for their safety must understand how conditions worsened. Questions about dangerousness must be formulated to elicit answers that give us hope for better days to come. The most fundamental question to be asked concerns the validity of the assumptions by which the law defines an offender as dangerous. From these assumptions accepted so widely and unquestioningly, policy emerges and decisions are made of great moment to the individuals to whom they are applied.

Assumptions and Predictions

In his closely argued essays on *The Future of Imprisonment*,[5] Morris proposes that dangerousness must be rejected as a basis for imposing a sentence of imprisonment. His review of the limited literature on the prediction of dangerousness is impressive and convincing. His argument is blessedly concise, and I shall not do it the injustice of a full recapitulation. What is relevant is his showing that social science does not have the capability to predict that any person, regardless of his previous record, will commit a violent act. Any effort to create such a system with the knowledge we now possess must make an unacceptable number of false positive predictions. Relying on the impressive study of dangerousness by Kozol, Boucher, and Garofalo, in which predictions of future dangerousness were made by clinicians examining the records of a large number of Massachusetts felons, Morris concludes that: "Even when a high risk group of convicted criminals is selected, and those carefully predicted as dangerous are detained, for every three so incarcerated there is only one who would in fact commit serious assaultive crime if all three were released."[6] This analysis leads Morris to conclude that society is not entitled to specify the restraint of any individual on the assumption that he is dangerous, even though in the past he has been guilty of violent acts.

There will never be a technique available to the courts that will enable a judge to sentence a violent offender in the light of certain prediction of future violence. The conquest of nature by the scientific method depends on human ability to discern regularities from which patterns can be discerned. The patterns lead to the prediction of probable events. Meteorologists have identified patterns by which rain can be predicted if certain observations can be made. Physicians have identified cell pathologies that will probably lead to death from cancer if they are allowed to develop without medical intervention. In these and many other cases, processes are under way that will bring about results which can be predicted by those who have studied their course.

A violent crime is not the result of a natural process. It is an event which occurs in the convergence of forces producing a unique situation. The drunk who is peaceable when sober but an uncontrollable brawler in his cups still has to find an antagonist, a situation where there is no one to restrain him, and a stimulus to arouse his aggression if he is to become an assaultive offender. In spite of speculations by hindsight, no one can identify the forces that accounted for Stephen Nash's hideous succession of meaningless homicides. The question of dangerousness did not arise in advance. In retrospect, it was and is impossible to reconstruct a basis for such a prediction.

There is no identifiable process that necessarily culminates in violence. The most that we can say is that the perusal of criminal dossiers will reveal that some people commit numerous acts of violence in the course of their criminal careers. Attempts to predict that any one of these previously violent people will commit another violent act will always end with false prophecies.

This situation is understandable. We do not have any paradigm that produces theories of behavior describing processes that lead to violence. This theoretical blank exists in spite of many paradigms relevant to aggressive behavior. Frustration-aggression, brain damage, subcultures relying on violence to support behavioral norms, and genetic abnormalities have all been invoked, but none has produced a model for prediction. As Morris points out, a statistical model that can predict violence from only one actor out of three, even when the past includes a record of violence, is not doing as well as a flip of a coin.

Yet there was Stephen Nash. There are always a few hundred like him scattered around the nation, though few cut such a swath of death. They must be considered dangerous and they must be so treated by the criminal justice system with the full approval of most of their fellow citizens. Nash went to the gas chamber. In the future, some like him will be put to death on the supposition that their very survival is a danger to the rest of society. The sentencing structure in most states is built to incarcerate dangerous criminals for longer than usual terms on the assumption of their presumed dangerousness. Criminal justice systems throughout history have been based, in part, on this concept of dangerousness for much longer than society has maintained prisons for punishment.

Society locks up criminals on the same assumptions that prompt the prudent to take precautions in handling explosives. Dynamite will detonate when carelessly handled, so those required to handle it take care to exercise the necessary safeguards. Some people are considered dangerous and the precaution taken with them is confinement to a cell.

A human being is not as simple as a stick of explosive material. Society is overprotected with respect to some dangerous offenders and underprotected with respect to others. Motives are mixed up; incarceration may simultaneously punish, deter, and incapacitate. The long term in prison may be imposed only to condemn a horrifying crime, but at the same time it will satisfy a prediction—however erroneous—that the criminal will do it again, given the opportunity.

Such considerations do not arise in the handling of explosives. Neither fairness to the individual charged with violent crime nor control for the benefit of society can result until the understanding of violence has progressed beyond the speculative stage on which laws and decisions are now based. Speculations are to be confirmed or rejected by a process of inquiry, the asking of really important questions. The Dangerous Offender Project begins with its version of these questions. We hope to end with a set of tentative answers, open to the challenge of confirmation and modification by events in police stations, courts, and jails across the country.

The Questions

I shall begin with an enumeration of the broad issues which, if resolved, would enable society to deal with the problems of dangerousness more effectively. Issues stated at this level of generality require disassembly into project-sized problems for data collection and analysis by social scientists. An implicit assumption in this discussion is the validity of the concept of dangerousness. The very idea rests on the proposition that some persons are more than ordinarily inclined to use violence for self-expression or as an instrument in gaining economic or social ends. To identify a population for study, the Dangerous Offender Project has arbitrarily defined a dangerous offender as one who has committed a violent crime on more than one occasion. Our studies will attempt to differentiate between such individuals and criminals who have limited themselves to one such act during their careers. We also intend to identify a population of offenders who appear to be "chronic" in the commission of such crimes, having four or more such offenses listed in their criminal histories. Conceivably, we will discover that nothing sets the dangerous offender apart from the rest of the criminal population except the frequency of his violence. We will then be left with the problem of allaying the fears and satisfying the skepticism of citizens who are certain that the quality of dangerousness does exist.

There are six broad questions with which scientific study can be usefully concerned:

1. Is there a taxonomy of dangerousness that will enable us to differentiate decision-making about violent offenders more accurately and equitably? Obviously, there is a profound and crucial difference between the offender whose violence is subcultural in origin and another whose central nervous system is so impaired as to render him prone to violent acts in provocative contexts. How far can a taxonomy usefully extend? What account, if any, should justice allow in making differential dispositions of offenders guilty of crimes with identical consequences to the victim but widely differing origins?

2. Can an offender's potential dangerousness be discriminated? Should psychologists continue to seek tests that can make such determinations? In spite of the reservations about statistical prediction that I have already recited in this disquisition, is it worth while to pursue this will-o'-the-wisp still further? If there can never be a better predictor of the future than the offender's past record, what ethical principles should be invoked to justify social control of persons whose past behavior inspires apprehensions for the future?

3. If society must define some offenders as dangerous by a criterion of law and practice, if not by scientifically established principles, what shall be done with them? How long shall they be detained, and what principles should govern the duration of their detention? What kinds of treatment shall the prison authorities offer them and why? What can be expected from a model program of control of dangerousness? Should society be satisfied with the protection afforded by the isolation of dangerous individuals in a fortress for some specified term, or should society insist that such individuals be released only when they no longer pose a threat to anyone?

4. Are there any biomedical or psychological interventions that can be accepted as compatible with the values of a free and moral society? Everyone has been properly horrified by Anthony Burgess's *Clockwork Orange*. Jessica Mitford has regaled critics of the criminal justice system with accounts of gothic

treatments once administered by some California correctional clinicians.[7] Obviously, there is a path that leads straight from scientific technique to abuses of the most horrifying character. Nevertheless, American correctional systems have for many years persisted in the operation of adjustment centers, punitive isolation, "deep six" units, and "doghouses" for the want of any better or more humane control of prisoners who are dangerous to everyone around them. There has been some outcry, but not nearly as much as is inspired by behavior modification programs, token economies, pharmacological interventions, or psychosurgery. Must there be an absolute prohibition of any such intervention, even though society tolerates the daily confrontation of the keeper with the kept at a constant level of threatened violence? To answer such a question, the facts must be known in relation to the irreversibility of medical interventions and the reality of informed consent to them. These issues are ideologically thorny, so much so that they are not well formulated. An acceptable ethical position must take account of the facts. On what basis can any irreversible intervention be morally tolerable? Under what conditions is a reversible or terminable intervention morally objectionable? Inherited and unexamined ideologies determine these positions now. Are they open to reasoned modification?

Most liberal thinkers lean to the position that informed consent cannot be given in a condition of duress. I am uncomfortable with this rule, but I am also uneasy about allowing exceptions to it. Nevertheless, if the offender in prison is not to be reduced to protracted irresponsibility, he must be encouraged to be responsible for himself, and such responsibility implies the power to give or withhold consent to treatment. Therefore, what are the boundaries within which he can be allowed to give consent? Will a better understanding of the extent of change from various forms of behavior modification lead to a better resolution of this issue? Empiricism will not settle the matter, but no satisfactory resolution can be expected without the development of the facts.

5. What kinds of intervention are appropriate for the dangerous juvenile offender? Conscience requires the law to discriminate the child offender from the adult. But what is a child, and what is to be done with him when he commits an act of violence? The law is shifting to a tougher position, but that does not mean it is making more sense. To lower the maximum age of juvenile court jurisdiction, to ease the process of binding over a child for adjudication in an adult court may satisfy advocates of increased severity, but these changes do not necessarily contribute to the solution of the problem. The reformatory for young adults is a risky place in which to work, and even riskier for those who have to live in it. The hazards are identical in the training school for the juvenile violent offender. Both reformatory and training school hold their captives for a while, but in the process may succeed only in making them worse. Are there any forms of treatment or control that can help these young people return safely to society before they are burnt-out, middle-aged ex-offenders?

6. What actions can a community take to reduce the level of violence? What

do the facts about violent behavior and its causes—as far as they can be known—indicate for relief from the fears that pervade American cities? What changes in the criminal justice system might give hope for more peaceful streets? What can be expected from the predictable processes of future social and demographic change?

The Idea of Danger

The *Oxford English Dictionary* defines danger as follows:

Danger [O.F. *dangier, danger:*—Late L. *dominiarium,* deriv. of *dominium,* f. *dominus,* lord, master. The sense development took place in O.F.: see Godefroy.]

1. Power of a lord or master, jurisdiction, dominion; power to dispose of, or to hurt or harm; esp. in phrase *in (a person's) danger,* within his power or at his mercy, sometimes meaning ... *In his debt or under obligation to him. Obs. or arch.*
> Chaucer: *Prol. 663:* In dawngere had he his owen gise The younger girles of the diocese.
> Shakespeare: *Merchant of Venice,* Act V, Sc. iv, 180; You stand within his danger, do you not?
2. Power (of a person, weapon, missile) to inflict physical injury.

Etymology is not always useful in the definition of terms for conceptual discourse; current usage, precisely defined, should establish the terms of analysis. I am indebted to Professor Theodore Sarbin for calling attention to the suggestive origins of the word with which we are most concerned.[8] Its derivation throws into sharp relief the history of the concept and its links to the idea of power and powerlessness. In the feudal centuries when the word came into being, all power resided in the lord, whose rule over his vassals was without legal curb. In the modern sense, all vassals were in danger of him. Only divine law restrained him from doing as he pleased with those over whom he ruled. The power of life and death was in his hands.

That power has been redistributed in modern times. Contemporary magnates do not enjoy the secular powers of the feudal lord but they can harm those below them in many ways, sometimes with little more restraint than in the Middle Ages, as when an employer deprives an employee of his livelihood. Technology and social change have conferred on the powerless a ready access to transitory powers of life and death, as every citizen who has lived in fear of robbery or rape knows all too well.

Established power in contemporary society is still in the hands of the mighty. Men and women who exercise legitimate authority are distant personages whose powers are sensed but not always understood by those over whose destinies they preside. Before them, the marginal individual in his daily frustrations and humiliations feels himself to be without autonomy. Small wonder that the seizure of a gun or the occasion of surprise can tempt him to take momentary power over a victim. He thus becomes a hoodlum lord, and all around him are vassals briefly in "danger" of him.

This wholly illegitimate power is not to be restrained by moral authority. In this age of uncertainty and pessimism, the most important source of civic insecurity is the sense that authority cannot be relied on as a guide to conduct. The philosophers, jurists, and teachers of the culture have suddenly become fallible. This loss can be attributed partly to the shocks of social change, partly to the anonymity that excuses contemporary people from the responsibilities of the citizen. In this social disorder, danger is diffused and violence festers. Knowledge, reason, and good will are all that the human race has to counter the random danger presented by the powerless. These resources must be applied to many other elements of the civic structure beyond the criminal justice system. Our police, courts, and prisons make up one of the least influential social institutions for the prevention and control of dangerousness.

What happened to Stephen Nash to make him the monster who died in the San Quentin gas chamber? No one will ever know. He was one of the least powerful of men, but it takes more than impotence to make a monster. Society must continue to ask and answer the questions that are raised by dangerous people like Stephen Nash. Once those like him are under the control of the courts and the prisons, official responsibilities are generated that are now discharged with many errors of commission and omission. Slowly our judges and wardens may improve their performance as they learn to examine their experience. Even more slowly we will learn how the children of the wretched and despised can be properly nurtured for harmless and hopeful lives.

Notes

1. George Jackson, *Soledad Brother* (New York: Bantam Books, 1970).

2. See, among many others, the following: American Friends Service Committee: *Struggle for Justice* (New York: Hill and Wang, 1971); Thomas Mathiesen, *The Politics of Abolition* (London: Martin Robertson, 1974); Thomas Murton, *The Dilemma of Prison Reform* (New York: Holt, Rinehart and Winston, 1976); Robert Sommer, *The End of Imprisonment* (New York: Oxford University Press, 1976).

3. *Toward a New Corrections Policy: Two Declarations of Principles*, The Academy for Contemporary Problems, 1974.

4. Edward Banfield, *The Unheavenly City* (Boston: Little, Brown and Co., 1968).

5. Norval Morris, *The Future of Imprisonment* (Chicago: University of Chicago Press, 1974).

6. Harry Kozol, Richard Boucher, and Ralph Garofalo, "The Diagnosis and Treatment of Dangerousness," *Crime and Delinquency*, 18: 371-392, 1972.

7. Jessica Mitford, *Kind and Usual Punishment: The Prison Business* (New York: Knopf, 1973).

8. Theodore Sarbin, "The Dangerous Individual," *The British Journal of Criminology*, 7: 285-295, 1967.

that George presented, the
nwide search for a private
Twelve well-known centers
m; he was too aggressive, too

completed two-and-one-half
mary psychiatric work-up, in
ther psychopathology. The
action of adolescence with
nce quotient of 81, but the
gh his School Achievement
hat score to the ninth-grade
f adolescence was "eclectic,"
iatric social worker and had
actional analysis and reality

was extremely aggressive. He
st of his peers. As he grew
im physically and were more
nt. He developed a crush on
ion was regarded as perfectly
, the emphasis was on his
the sexual elements in his
e relationships with other

mber 1976. George thought
d he acknowledged that the
had learned all he could at
lease were to be deferred it
uthority opposed his return
ne. Extended negotiation led

m's inadequacies in dealing
ven when his problems are
dianapolis had neither the
s to meet the serious need
George's delinquent career
other city is better provided.
en through the provision of
ple, strangers to him, were
gardless of the success of his
his life with an indigestible
ed.

2

The Importance of Being George: Unanswered Questions About the Dangerous Juvenile Offender

John P. Conrad

In 1972 Wolfgang, Figlio, and Sellin published the pivotal study *Delinquency in a Birth Cohort.*[1] It is not an easy book to read, filled as it is with tables and their explication, an esoteric statistical method, and a sober disinclination to adorn an empirical report with examples or speculation. In spite of the academic murk of its exposition, from the first the study has enjoyed a *succès d'estime* that is partly attributable to a troubling confirmation of the folk wisdom of the police.

The finding for which the study has become famous is simple. Among many other questions, Wolfgang and his colleagues were interested in discovering what proportion of boys in a metropolitan setting was to any extent identified as delinquent. To settle this question, they assembled a "birth cohort" consisting of 9945 males: all the boys born in Philadelphia in 1945 who lived in that city between their tenth and eighteenth years. With the cooperation of the police and the courts, they assembled the delinquent history, if any, of each boy, along with school records, indexes of socioeconomic status, race, intelligence quotient, and other variables generally considered to be significant for such an analysis.

Of the total sample, 3469, or 34.9 percent, had been charged with one or more acts of delinquency. The sum of these delinquencies was 10,214, of which 5305, or 51.9 percent, were committed by 627 "chronic recidivists," a term limited for this study to boys who were guilty of five or more offenses. Thus about 18 percent of the delinquents accounted for slightly more than half the delinquencies. Put another way, 6.3 percent of the boys studied were responsible for about half the offenses committed by the whole cohort.

The investigators found that the chronic recidivists were more likely to be nonwhite than white, were more likely to be lower on the socioeconomic scale than their less delinquent peers, averaged lower in intelligence quotients and school performance, and were more likely to commit serious offenses. The finding leads to the recommendation that " . . . any social intervention that could stop these delinquent cases before they go beyond their fourth delinquency would decrease significantly the number of offenses committed by a birth cohort. Such social action, if concentrated on the lower SES chronic offenders, would not only reduce the amount but also the seriousness of the offenses committed."[2]

This conclusion coincides with the contention of most police chiefs that if a small number of hoodlums could be swept off the streets and kept under firm

13

control, law and order could be re-established an
neither researchers nor police have accompanied tl
tions for an intervention and control model. It wo
draft a statute authorizing protracted detention
followed, probably, by appropriately extended si
prescription about the kind of treatment that woul
so detained, nor on what terms their surveillance v
all these young people would have to be released eve
problem suggest that it is likely that recidivists will r
are notably lacking that their sequestration in a you
further offenses less likely.

The dangerous juvenile offender is included
cohort; it cannot be assumed from the Wolfgang
recidivists were dangerous in the restricted sense that
a violent crime. Some dangerous young people
chronicity. But however many dangerous juvenile
remain on the street because of three elements of the
favor their freedom.

First, the law is written to protect the rights of t
guilty, no matter what the evidence against him
solicitous of the accused juvenile, partly because of tl
of any juvenile before the criminal court, and part
unwillingness to propel a child into the rigors of the c
all the implications for future criminality that
experience of arrest, detention, and trial. Second, tl
too overwhelmed with the volume of defendants o
with their caseloads or to assess specific cases in th
Third, the correctional systems, also overwhelmed v
the expertise nor the program models for effectiv
rehabilitating, the dangerous juvenile offender.[3]

The consequence of these inadequacies is vast da
in juvenile justice. No one has the basis for estimat
system's effectiveness in the control and deterrenc
attributable to a system that, in most communi
nominally. The harm done to individual victims is defi
power to make whole.

The difficulties inherent in the demand for contro
offender are not readily apparent in statistics suc
Wolfgang and his colleagues. Obvious though they ma
in this introduction, their remedy has been beyond tl
In the following pages, I shall recount two case hi
realities confronting the system. I shall end by offerin
a strategy to achieve better management of a numer
social destructiveness far exceeding its human dimensio

better plan. Realizing the formidable difficulties
court took the unusual step of initiating a nati
residential treatment facility to undertake his care
were queried, but not one was willing to accept hi
hostile for the kinds of programs they had to offer.

Committed to a youth training facility, George
years of secure custodial care. There was the custc
which he was found to be without psychosis or
diagnosis of record was "unsocialized aggressive
depressive tendencies." He tested for an intellige
psychometrist thought he seemed brighter. Altho
Test on admission was 2.5, he was able to elevate
level. His treatment for his unsocialized aggression c
meaning that he had regular interviews with a psyc
group treatment employing the concepts of trans
therapy.

When George was first received, his behavior
got into many fights, and his size intimidated mc
older, his fellow residents began to catch up with l
of a match for him, so the brawls became less frequ
one of the female school teachers, but this infatua
natural and caused no alarm. In group treatmen
"here-and-now" problems. Nothing was said abou
offenses. The stress was placed on his aggressi
residents.

His first prerelease hearing took place in Nove
himself ready to go home to his foster parents, ai
institutional program had helped him. He said he
school and from treatment and added that if his r
could be only for punishment. The Indiana Youth
to that state and suggested placement in a group hoi
to placement in a group home in still another state.

This record illustrates the juvenile justice sys
with the exceptionally serious juvenile offender,
recognizable in advance of a coming crisis. Ii
professional resources nor the institutional faciliti
that the juvenile court saw at least a year before
reached its grotesque climax. To our knowledge, no
Because the community was unable to help him, e
minimum controls, a considerable number of pe
subjected to distressing and painful experiences. R
future plans, George will have to live the rest of
burden of guilt and shame for the crimes he commit

The Importance of Being George: Unanswered Questions About the Dangerous Juvenile Offender

John P. Conrad

In 1972 Wolfgang, Figlio, and Sellin published the pivotal study *Delinquency in a Birth Cohort*.[1] It is not an easy book to read, filled as it is with tables and their explication, an esoteric statistical method, and a sober disinclination to adorn an empirical report with examples or speculation. In spite of the academic murk of its exposition, from the first the study has enjoyed a *succès d'estime* that is partly attributable to a troubling confirmation of the folk wisdom of the police.

The finding for which the study has become famous is simple. Among many other questions, Wolfgang and his colleagues were interested in discovering what proportion of boys in a metropolitan setting was to any extent identified as delinquent. To settle this question, they assembled a "birth cohort" consisting of 9945 males: all the boys born in Philadelphia in 1945 who lived in that city between their tenth and eighteenth years. With the cooperation of the police and the courts, they assembled the delinquent history, if any, of each boy, along with school records, indexes of socioeconomic status, race, intelligence quotient, and other variables generally considered to be significant for such an analysis.

Of the total sample, 3469, or 34.9 percent, had been charged with one or more acts of delinquency. The sum of these delinquencies was 10,214, of which 5305, or 51.9 percent, were committed by 627 "chronic recidivists," a term limited for this study to boys who were guilty of five or more offenses. Thus about 18 percent of the delinquents accounted for slightly more than half the delinquencies. Put another way, 6.3 percent of the boys studied were responsible for about half the offenses committed by the whole cohort.

The investigators found that the chronic recidivists were more likely to be nonwhite than white, were more likely to be lower on the socioeconomic scale than their less delinquent peers, averaged lower in intelligence quotients and school performance, and were more likely to commit serious offenses. The finding leads to the recommendation that " . . . any social intervention that could stop these delinquent cases before they go beyond their fourth delinquency would decrease significantly the number of offenses committed by a birth cohort. Such social action, if concentrated on the lower SES chronic offenders, would not only reduce the amount but also the seriousness of the offenses committed."[2]

This conclusion coincides with the contention of most police chiefs that if a small number of hoodlums could be swept off the streets and kept under firm control, law and order could be re-established and maintained. Unfortunately, neither researchers nor police have accompanied this conclusion with specifications for an intervention and control model. It would doubtless be possible to draft a statute authorizing protracted detention for the chronic recidivist, followed, probably, by appropriately extended surveillance. We are given no prescription about the kind of treatment that would be provided for the youths so detained, nor on what terms their surveillance would be terminated. Clearly all these young people would have to be released eventually, but the terms of the problem suggest that it is likely that recidivists will recidivate, and the assurances are notably lacking that their sequestration in a youth training school will make further offenses less likely.

The dangerous juvenile offender is included in this small sector of the cohort; it cannot be assumed from the Wolfgang data that all 627 chronic recidivists were dangerous in the restricted sense that they were likely to commit a violent crime. Some dangerous young people stop short of Wolfgang's chronicity. But however many dangerous juvenile offenders there are, they remain on the street because of three elements of the juvenile justice system that favor their freedom.

First, the law is written to protect the rights of the accused until he is found guilty, no matter what the evidence against him may be. It is particularly solicitous of the accused juvenile, partly because of the diminished responsibility of any juvenile before the criminal court, and partly because of the society's unwillingness to propel a child into the rigors of the criminal justice system, with all the implications for future criminality that are involved in the early experience of arrest, detention, and trial. Second, the courts in large cities are too overwhelmed with the volume of defendants of all ages to deal promptly with their caseloads or to assess specific cases in the light of full information. Third, the correctional systems, also overwhelmed with numbers, have neither the expertise nor the program models for effectively controlling, let alone rehabilitating, the dangerous juvenile offender.[3]

The consequence of these inadequacies is vast damage to public confidence in juvenile justice. No one has the basis for estimating the impairment of the system's effectiveness in the control and deterrence of delinquency that is attributable to a system that, in most communities, is functioning only nominally. The harm done to individual victims is definable but beyond society's power to make whole.

The difficulties inherent in the demand for control of the dangerous juvenile offender are not readily apparent in statistics such as those produced by Wolfgang and his colleagues. Obvious though they may seem when presented as in this introduction, their remedy has been beyond the wisdom of criminology. In the following pages, I shall recount two case histories that illustrate the realities confronting the system. I shall end by offering the essential elements of a strategy to achieve better management of a numerically small problem with social destructiveness far exceeding its human dimensions.

George Clancy: Present but not Accounted for

From time to time every city produces a youth and an occasion to remind all who may be concerned of the municipal inadequacy to cope with the graver forms of personal pathology. For Indianapolis, George Clancy (fictitious name) was that youth, and the occasion took place in October 1974.

George was a fourteen-year-old black, six feet two inches tall and strongly built. He had been a well-known problem to the community for at least three years. On that autumn evening in 1974 he and two associates, one an adult, the other a minor but older than George, made an armed foray into a middle-class white neighborhood. With a shotgun, they entered and robbed three retail establishments. They emptied cash registers and, at the point of their weapon, forced proprietors and customers to disrobe. Later George was to explain that it was his idea that the confusion and embarrassment caused by the nudity would delay the alarm. The tactics worked perfectly in the first store. In the second, George was aroused by the nakedness of one of his female victims and raped her. In the third store, he tried to force a male customer to rape one of the women present. When he refused, George clubbed him and shoved the barrel of his shotgun into the woman's vagina.

The three culprits were arrested. The unusually repulsive brutality of the crimes made George's case a *cause célèbre* in the Indianapolis newspapers. George's name and record were made public. The press designated him as a "monster man" because of his unusual size for his age and the disgusting character of his crimes. In disposing of the case, the juvenile court judge expressed the hope that he would be restrained behind bars for many years to come. Because of the extensive publicity and because there were no facilities in Indiana with sufficiently secure custody, he was placed in a youth training school in another state.

Born to a white couple, it became apparent in early childhood that George had been fathered by a black. His legal father deserted, his mother was unable to cope, and her children were dispersed to foster homes. George was placed with an older black couple whose youngest son was thirteen years older than he. He was brought up with his foster parents' grandchildren, some of them about the same age.

At the age of twelve, George was taken into custody by the police on the complaint of a foster sister, who said he had fought with and broken the jaw of her son. George was sent to a group home for six months, then returned home, where he seems to have been out of effective control. Smoking marijuana and shoplifting to support purchases, he seems to have begun his career as a robber at about this time. He boasts that he robbed several filling stations every week, but if he did, he escaped arrest. After about a year of this uncontrolled behavior, he was caught during the burglary of a neighbor's home. The juvenile court placed him in a group home in which all the other boys were white. There were daily fights, most of which George won. The group home placement was for lack of a better plan. Realizing the formidable difficulties that George presented, the court took the unusual step of initiating a nationwide search for a private residential treatment facility to undertake his care. Twelve well-known centers were queried, but not one was willing to accept him; he was too aggressive, too hostile for the kinds of programs they had to offer.

Committed to a youth training facility, George completed two-and-one-half years of secure custodial care. There was the customary psychiatric work-up, in which he was found to be without psychosis or other psychopathology. The diagnosis of record was "unsocialized aggressive reaction of adolescence with depressive tendencies." He tested for an intelligence quotient of 81, but the psychometrist thought he seemed brighter. Although his School Achievement Test on admission was 2.5, he was able to elevate that score to the ninth-grade level. His treatment for his unsocialized aggression of adolescence was "eclectic," meaning that he had regular interviews with a psychiatric social worker and had group treatment employing the concepts of transactional analysis and reality therapy.

When George was first received, his behavior was extremely aggressive. He got into many fights, and his size intimidated most of his peers. As he grew older, his fellow residents began to catch up with him physically and were more of a match for him, so the brawls became less frequent. He developed a crush on one of the female school teachers, but this infatuation was regarded as perfectly natural and caused no alarm. In group treatment, the emphasis was on his "here-and-now" problems. Nothing was said about the sexual elements in his offenses. The stress was placed on his aggressive relationships with other residents.

His first prerelease hearing took place in November 1976. George thought himself ready to go home to his foster parents, and he acknowledged that the institutional program had helped him. He said he had learned all he could at school and from treatment and added that if his release were to be deferred it could be only for punishment. The Indiana Youth Authority opposed his return to that state and suggested placement in a group home. Extended negotiation led to placement in a group home in still another state.

This record illustrates the juvenile justice system's inadequacies in dealing with the exceptionally serious juvenile offender, even when his problems are recognizable in advance of a coming crisis. Indianapolis had neither the professional resources nor the institutional facilities to meet the serious need that the juvenile court saw at least a year before George's delinquent career reached its grotesque climax. To our knowledge, no other city is better provided. Because the community was unable to help him, even through the provision of minimum controls, a considerable number of people, strangers to him, were subjected to distressing and painful experiences. Regardless of the success of his future plans, George will have to live the rest of his life with an indigestible burden of guilt and shame for the crimes he committed.

His predicament is a standing challenge to juvenile corrections. Irresponsibility occasioned his begetting; more irresponsibility cast him into a ruinous childhood from which a good outcome was improbable. In many juvenile courts, his early contacts would have been routinely processed because his behavior would have been seen as unremarkable against the backdrop of the ordinary court caseload. The Indianapolis court was sensitive enough to detect an unusual and serious problem but powerless to intervene constructively.

It is understandable that in the volume of business transacted in the juvenile justice system, the first consideration must be to create a process that makes the appropriate distinctions among the more common kinds of cases appearing before the court and to be disposed of by commitment to a suitable element of the correctional apparatus. It is easy to understand the refusal of the agencies the court queried to accept George for service. None of them were established to care for a boy with such formidable problems; none of them could take the chance of disrupting their programs by an attempt to provide for an oversized, combative youth with long experience outside of effective adult control.

The point is that neither social service nor correctional control is equipped to provide effective service for such a boy until a crisis requires the state to impose maximum security control in a total institution. Accumulated clinical experience with similar youths has not crystallized into guidance for treatment and decision-making. Until reliable resources for early treatment become available, the occasional George Clancy who shocks a whole city will be handled ineffectually and aimlessly rather than as a child in need of help. There must be a better response to George Clancy than to wait until he becomes a monster, eligible for the control of a juvenile institution. The conceptual basis for such a response does not seem to be even in sight at this point in the development of the helping services.

How the System Lost George Adorno

The national press has not muted its concern about the inadequacies of all elements of the juvenile justice system. The media of New York City have been especially attentive to the problem. Accounts are regularly given of violent recidivists turned loose to offend again and more grievously. The themes are persistent in their recurrence. The disorganized squalor of the ghetto, the overwhelmed courts, and the ineffectual correctional programs constitute a desperately vicious cycle that inevitably drags the juvenile into crises from which nobody can extricate him. The system's functioning, as described to the public, inevitably adds to the terror of the city but never to the offender's regeneration. The repetitive pattern of inevitable tragedy is surely exaggerated, but the facts for realistic perspective are hard to come by. What is certain is that distressing examples abound, and we have not learned enough from them to prevent their frequent occurrence.

A recent case is that of George Adorno, whose history has been reported in the popular press.[4] In February 1977, at the age of eighteen, George was arrested for homicide, the second such crime with which he has been charged in his short life (although he has been suspected of six). Each charge arose from the killing of a cab driver he allegedly enticed to a lonely street late at night to rob. The first charge was brought into the family court when George was fifteen, but it was dismissed by the judge on the grounds that his mother, then on a visit in Puerto Rico, had not been present during his police investigation. Between that time and the second murder with which he was charged, he had been arrested and tried for robbery, committed to the Elmira Reformatory, and released eighteen months before the expiration of his term. Apparently, he had been a reasonably compliant inmate during his incarceration at the reformatory; there is no other apparent reason for his unusually early release. There had been earlier removals from the streets of Harlem. At Warwick, a facility of the New York State Division for Youth, where George spent about a year when he was fourteen, he was allowed home on weekend passes. During these respites from confinement he was arrested twice for robbery on successive weekends, but on each occasion he was able to return to the facility without his keepers becoming aware that he had come to police attention. His failure to appear in family court because of his confinement at Warwick was natural enough; the court did not have enough warrant officers to find out where he was so that he could be picked up. Finally released entirely from custody, George was involved, according to the magazine story, in a series of murders—and no disposition was made for any of them. At the time of this writing, he is awaiting trial for the sixth murder of which he has been in one way or another suspected.

Even in the megalopolis there are not many like George Adorno. He is illiterate, devoted to his mother and sisters, thoroughly versed in the realities of the criminal justice system as it operates in New York City, and unable to make any accommodation of his impulses of the moment to the most elementary rights of others, even the right to life itself. There is no great difficulty in formulating a psychological diagnosis or in arriving at a theory to account for his behavior. Drawing from the work of such clinicians as Marguerite Warren or Carl Jesness, it is not difficult to think of a treatment plan that in an effective system might have succeeded with George at an earlier stage, long before his reputation included merciless homicide.

As with George Clancy, however, the system lacked the resources for treatment, or even the will to treat. Nicholas Pileggi, author of the *New York* article, reports that the staff of the Division for Youth is convinced that rehabilitation does not work and that it is impossible to distinguish between those in its custody who are dangerous and those who are not. A kind of anarchy has permeated the decision-making echelons. Faced with a child like George, the system's incapacity begins with its lack of accountability. The immense amount of work to be done excuses the gravest error in judgment. Who can blame a hard-pressed judge or probation officer for making a lenient decision so that a boy can return to his mother? The blame becomes more difficult to assign when every element of court service is short-handed and the basic information is so hard to obtain.

The strain on the court because of the crushing load of work is compounded by an even more serious deficiency: The prevalent belief that rehabilitation does not "work" has excused many correctional workers from working. It is difficult to censure them. The clinical theorists have not been able to furnish them with an alternative doctrine of intervention. To officials faced with the notion that efforts to treat are futile and the companion notion that efforts to control may be needlessly oppressive, an anarchic policy of inaction is reasonable enough.

There is a third deterrent to positive action to control boys like George Adorno. Someone has to pick him up when he is wanted, and someone else has to visit his home regularly if he is receiving community-based services. Even the doughtiest police officer may have qualms about an assignment to call at a barrio tenement to arrest a boy known for the ferocity of his responses to interference. The assignment is even more unattractive for a probation officer, even an officer who lives in the community and knows it well.

For all these reasons, the system functions only nominally in many metropolitan situations. The human interactions on which its success must depend occur randomly, if at all, and almost never in the case of boys like George Adorno. The consequences are horrifying, and not to be remedied by merely adjusting organization charts, lines of authority, and work flow channels.

A New Anomie?

Do George Clancy and George Adorno represent a new phenomenon? Some observers think so, arguing that the amorality of the streets has created a new kind of anomie born of the knowledge that what one does has no predictable consequences. Whether this belief is valid or not, whether these alarming youths are precursors of a new, mutant criminality does not immediately matter. They may be merely the familiar textbook psychopaths, brutalized by the special influences of racism and welfare dependence. The point is that no one knows what to do with them. As Wolfgang and his associates have shown, the juvenile justice system's success in inducing the desistance of recidivist juveniles is unimpressive.[5] The system's power to intervene early enough to prevent the horrifying careers of these two Georges is limited to the mild restraints of supervision in the community. No service is in sight that can reliably change such a child, even when he is recognized early, as was the case with George Clancy. A theory of treatment on which such a service could be built has not emerged from the doctrinal disputes of the social scientists and the psychiatrists. The ordinary clinical management of the system has all it can do to keep the daily workload moving; experimentation for the benefit of the unusually dangerous juvenile is beyond the resources allowed the system or, indeed, its general assignment from the state.

Faced with the system's impotence, many reasonable people incline to the long-term incapacitation of such offenders in the absence of any better strategy. The eloquent arguments of van den Haag[6] are explicit on this pragmatic recommendation. Yet the arguments against such a course are powerful. The victims of these aimless terrorists will still be victimized. The facilities for the incarceration of such children for the terms that the exponents of protracted custody have in mind do not exist, will be extraordinarily difficult to staff if they are created, and under any circumstances they will be costly to maintain. Finally, it is hard to foresee the regeneration of the juvenile justice system in a form and with resources capable of catching, trying, and keeping serious delinquents in sufficient numbers to be credibly deterrent.

Must the answer be the insidious counsel of despair? Not at all. Where society must overwhelm its criminal justice systems with numbers that the systems were not designed to handle, George Clancy and George Adorno assume an importance and a significance that is easily misinterpreted. In a sense, they are indeed young monsters. Brought into the world more by accident than by hope, they are nurtured in the ambiance of irresponsibility and hostility. Their parents are denounced as lazy cheats or written off as redundant. They come by their monstrosity honestly enough; the welfare system that kept them alive has taught them that the only way to get what one wants is to take it, even by extreme intimidation.

The answer to George Clancy and George Adorno can be found only by changing the communities of despair from which they came into communities in which hope is a realistic virtue. Until the men and women who live in the most terrible sections of our bankrupt cities can be helped to put their neighborhoods into a state of responsible community, no juvenile justice system is imaginable that can deal with these two important young men named George.

Notes

1. Marvin E. Wolfgang, Robert M. Figlio, and Thorstein Sellin, *Delinquency in a Birth Cohort* (Chicago: University of Chicago Press, 1972).

2. Ibid., p. 105.

3. Clemens Bartollas, Stuart J. Miller, and Simon Dinitz, *Juvenile Victimization: The Institutional Paradox* (New York: Sage Publications, 1976).

4. Nicholas Pileggi, "Inside the Juvenile-Justice System: How Fifteen-Year-Olds Get Away With Murder," New York, 13 June 1977, pp. 36-44.

5. Wolfgang, Figlio, and Sellin.

6. Ernest van den Haag, *Punishing Criminals* (New York: Basic Books, 1975), pp. 241-251.

3

Chronically Antisocial Offenders

Simon Dinitz

This chapter reviews a massive conceptual confusion. From the beginning of psychiatric nosology, clinicians have needed a term to describe and a paradigm for the treatment of the impulsive, unpredictable, conscienceless men and women whose lives exhibit patterns of conscienceless predation on persons around them. In the beginning they were called "constitutional psychopathic inferiors." The terminology has shifted from period to period. Sometimes the condition has been called "psychopathy," sometimes "sociopathy," and recent literature leans to the use of "antisocial personality."

Whatever the term, both clinicians and criminal justice professionals recognize characteristics that are shared by a wide spectrum of offenders, relatively few of whom are violent. Conversely, an unknown but probably modest fraction of the chronically violent offenders fit the clinical criteria of antisocial personalities. There are many unknowns in these estimates, but no serious research in the problems of dangerousness can fail to confront the baffling issue of the antisocial personality. The characteristics attributed to the clinical model are those that immediately strike the observer in accounting for Stephen Nash, Richard Speck, Charles Manson, and other villains of our time.

Whether knaves or buffoons, drifters or drudges, pillars of the community or ne'er-do-wells, these antisocial personalities wear a "mask of sanity." Behind the mask lies a hostility to the human environment that finds expression in actions of mendacity and aggression. We can understand the actions of the terrorist with political goals, or of the kidnapper who hopes to gain riches, or of the burglar, robber, or thief. But what of a Stephen Nash? How do we account for the dispassionate killer who coolly told us how he kidnapped and drowned a six-year-old girl? What moves the long-term inhabitant of solitary confinement who asked for only thirty minutes on the yard—no more, he assured us—to kill a man who had offended him years ago?

Other examples abound. Everyone who has worked in maximum security prisons has encountered apparently rational people who had committed macabre crimes on pure whim. The social scientist and the clinician do not understand them well, but the suspicion that there is a link between the antisocial personality and the dangerous offender is a plausible hypothesis. Neither clinical experience nor psychometric techniques enable us to predict the fearful course of their lives nor to account for them after the course is run. But on this plausible hypothesis we now turn to a review of what is known or seems to be known about the men and women who fall into this most elusive of psychiatric categories.

21

Chronically Antisocial Offenders

Antisocial personality is a clinical disorder whose course, mechanisms, and etiology remain unknown. Genetic, physiological, interactional, and socio-cultural etiologies have been advanced to explain this intractable behavioral disorder. None has resulted in the most convincing proof: successful treatment. Psychopathy is not recognized as a form of mental illness in Anglo-American legal codes. From the M'Naghten Rule to the American Law Institute Model Penal Code—a period exceeding 100 years—the psychopath has been held to be fully responsible for his conduct. As in many other areas, the law and psychiatry are at odds. The 1952 Diagnostic and Statistical Manual of the American Psychiatric Association described these maladaptive persons as:

... chronically anti-social individuals who are always in trouble, profiting neither from experience nor punishment and maintaining no real loyalty to any person, group, or code. They are frequently callous and hedonistic, showing marked emotional immaturity with lack of sense of responsibility, lack of judgment, and an ability to rationalize their behavior so that it appears warranted, reasonable and justified.[1]

Neither the second (1968) edition of the American Psychiatric Association's Diagnostic and Statistical Manual of Mental Disorders nor the 1969 APA glossary mention such traditional and now obsolete terms as "sociopathy" and "psychopathy." This most recent change in classification replaces "sociopathy" with "antisocial personality," the latter described as follows:

This term [antisocial personality] is reserved for individuals who are basically unsocialized and whose behavior pattern brings them repeatedly into conflict with society. They are incapable of significant loyalty to individuals, groups, or social values. They are grossly selfish, callous, irresponsible, impulsive, and unable to feel guilt or to learn from experience. Frustration tolerance is low. They tend to blame others or offer plausible rationalizations for their behavior. . . .[2]

Once generally called psychopathy,[3] constitutional psychopathic state, and psychopathic personality, sociopathy has been attributed to a variety of causes.[4]

Available clinical evidence indicates that psychopaths may constitute from 1 to 3 percent of all adults of both sexes. In addition, based on prison classification data, at least 20 percent of the adult correctional population in the United States have antisocial personalities.[5] Whatever the true prevalence, antisocial personality is an economically and socially expensive mental disorder. Psychopathy has been found to be associated with a shortened life span[6] and an unstable family life; it is a burden of conduct that, when not criminal, is often predatory or destructive. Chronically antisocial persons tend to resist efforts to resocialize them; they are often disruptive to the point of negating such efforts for the remaining 80 percent of the prisoners.

This 20-percent institutional prevalence estimate, which is in line with recent findings (including my own), has been accepted for years as reasonably adequate. But like estimates of most other psychiatric problems, there is no way to ascertain the true prevalence since clinicians differ markedly in their definition of antisocial personality and even of the more inclusive category of character disorders. Disregarding the actual prevalence, antisocial personality is frequently used as a diagnostic label, especially when other diagnoses are inappropriate and when it serves institutional and system needs, e.g., in delaying the granting of parole or warehousing a recalcitrant prisoner in a prison hospital for the criminally insane.

Whatever the etiology of psychopathy, the disruption of the modern family, the increased geographic mobility, the "eclipse" of a sense of community, the emergence of the female-headed household, and the social disorganization brought about by urbanization and industrialization have surely exacerbated the problem. The chronically antisocial offender creates problems for the community; the city brings out the worst in the psychopath. The spiral effect is to be seen in "children who hate,"[7] the "core" members of gangs,[8] and the changing composition of the prison population. Experienced correctional managers are disturbed by this trend and confess that they are unable to deal constructively with these highly disruptive inmates; at best they can only contain them.

Many clinicians believe that the condition is probably an irreversible disorder; there is also consensus that little headway has been made in devising effective management and control techniques. In general, they also believe that no effective therapy exists and, even worse, that such chronically antisocial offenders are not amenable to treatment.[9]

Although character disorders have been studied extensively by clinicians and psychometricians, none of the basic questions have been answered.[10] Is sociopathy a disorder or a series of problems that, for lack of a conceptual framework, are lumped together as a residual classification? What are the fundamental attributes of this category? What is its etiology and progression? What do we know about it clinically, physiologically, psychologically, sociologically? Are there distinct types of sociopathy? If so, how can they be distinguished? What interventions have been used? What has been the outcome of various specific programs, e.g., creating a structured environment, milieu therapy, drug treatment? Assuming that clinicians can identify a Manson, an Oswald, a Clancy, how should they respond to their potential for harm? Is society justified in isolating them before they commit their dreadful crimes? On what criteria? For how long? Even if no treatment is possible because of our limited knowledge?

Early Formulations

The contemporary conception of the antisocial personality has evolved from formulations advanced by numerous investigators, most of whom derived their theories and insights from clinical experience.

Pinel is credited with first describing this phenomenon in modern terms.[11] His classification and description of *manie sans delire* (mania without delirium), while mixing a variety of disorders, dealt with this previously unexplained phenomenon. His tripartite classification (impulsive insanity and moral idiocy, hypomania, and melancholia activa) broadened the conception of mental illness and led the assault on the prevailing opinion that the intellect is always involved in mental illness.

The American psychiatrist Benjamin Rush expressed similar ideas as early as 1812, using terms like "moral alienation," "defective organization of moral faculties," and "deranged will."[12] While postulating a special moral sense in accordance with cognitive psychology, Rush, like Pinel, recognized that mental illness may involve other than intellectual faculties. Rush, incidentally, was also a partisan of phrenology.

These formulations influenced the English physician J.C. Prichard.[13] His comprehensive descriptions of sociopathy (psychopathy), under the titles of "moral insanity" and "moral imbecility," drew attention to states characterized by an affective and feeling disorder, rather than of understanding and intellectual defect. Although his description of nonintellectual "insanity" was a bold step in the classification of mental diseases, Prichard classified all disorders on the basis of symptomatology and consequently included states other than antisocial personality.

Garofalo, one of the major founders of positivist criminology, attempted to evade the issue of moral insanity by suggesting that biological factors might be present:

Should [such moral anomalies as the sociopath] be regarded as a new nosologic form—the moral insanity of English writers? The existence of this form of alienation is questionable, to say the least. In spite of utmost efforts to discover traces of insanity, one is often obliged to admit that the individual under examination possesses an intelligence which leaves nothing to be desired, that he exhibits no nosologic symptom, unless it be the absence of a moral sense, and that, to quote a French physician, whatever be the subject's unity of mind, "the psychic keyboard has one true note and only one."[14]

Garofalo casually added that "these children (are) born with ferocious instincts."

For criminals exhibiting chronic imprudence, lack of insight, moral insensibility, and complete indifference to shame, Garofalo substituted the term "constitutional inferiority" for "moral insanity."

Lombroso, the father of modern positivist criminology and a forensic psychiatrist, embraced the concept of the chronically antisocial offender as a moral imbecile.[15] He characterized him as impervious to guilt, highly aggressive, impulsive, boastful, and particularly insensitive to social criticism and physical pain. Incidentally, recent empirical evidence suggests that the psychopath does show a higher threshold for pain.[16] Lombroso wanted such persons placed in asylums: "At first sight this proposition seems absurd. . . . But proper attention has not been paid to the fact that it is just such . . . cases, intermediate between reason and insanity, in which, therefore, the criminal asylums are most useful and of most service in guaranteeing the public safety."[17]

The influence of the Italian positivist school of Lombroso and Garofalo and their disciples still persists a century later. There lingers the implicit conception that "criminal man" is an evolutionary throwback, a monster identifiable by physical and psychic anomalies, a beastly sort beyond treatment and correction. Many of the characteristics of the antisocial personality were first enunciated by Lombroso and Garofalo. As will be seen, these same attributes inform clinical thinking today. Hervey Cleckley's catalogue of symptoms (the definitive statement on this matter as of 1977) is chiefly an update of some of this early thinking.

Partridge first introduced the term sociopath, suggesting that this disorder resulted from defective socialization.[18] Applying psychoanalytic theory, he located the sociopath's maladjustment in the developmental process. From a study of 50 subjects, he argued that the sociopath fails to progress through the stages of normal childhood development and retains adjustment techniques common to early life. Partridge used arcane Freudian terminology and concepts in describing this disorder as a permanently fixed concentration on oral needs. His studies led him to conclude that the sociopathic personality "is a persistent behavior pattern or tendency in which there is usually excessive demand . . . which when there is a failure of direct or immediate satisfaction, is reacted to by a tendency to develop characteristic ways of dominating situations; by emotional displays we call tantrums, by sulks; by running away. . . ."[19]

Thompson had a somewhat similar conception.[20] To him, sociopathy involved a personality deviation characterized by an inability to adjust adequately and consistently to social standards. Thompson maintained that this deviation stems from a basic mental defect that renders the sufferer incapable of developing an adequate sense of time, particularly with regard to self. Lack of guilt, insufficient judgment, impulsiveness, and inability to profit from experience are secondary symptoms.

Henderson used the term "psychopathic state" to refer to the antisocial personality, and he included three groups under this rubric: the predominantly aggressive, the predominantly passive or inadequate, and the predominantly creative.[21] The third state suggests that the genius is a variant of the sociopath.[22] This sort of typology reflects the flawed reasoning typical of so much of the past and present literature. The increasing disrepute of clinicians as thinkers and healers may be attributed, in part, to such nosologies. At any rate, Henderson described the sociopath as unstable, explosive, and egocentric. Psychic immaturity is the prime feature of his condition:

He cannot accept things as they are; he is unable to fit into the life of the herd, but tends to lead an independent, individualistic type of existence with no thought or feeling for his family, his friends, or his country. He is blunted emotionally . . . for a time he may prove charming. . . . For some inscrutable reason he fails to grow up, he remains at the level of a primitive savage with a distaste for reasoning and an "impermeability to experience". . . . The judicial, deciding, selecting process described as intelligence, and the energizing, emotivating, driving powers called character, are not working in harmony.[23]

Cleckley has provided the most recent and widely used checklist of symptoms of antisocial sociopaths, maintaining that they are distinguishable, deeply-rooted clinical entities.[24] The disorder adversely affects interpersonal relations and is demonstrated best when sociopaths confront problems of everyday living.

Disdaining parsimony, Cleckley describes the antisocial sociopath in these terms:

1. Superficial charm and good intelligence.
2. Absence of delusions and other signs of irrational thinking.
3. Absence of nervousness and other psychoneurotic manifestations.
4. Unreliability.
5. Untruthfulness and insincerity.
6. Lack of remorse or shame.
7. Inadequately motivated anti-social behavior.
8. Poor judgment and failure to learn by experience.
9. Pathologic egocentricity and incapacity for love.
10. General poverty of major affective relations.
11. Specific loss of insight.
12. Unresponsiveness in interpersonal behavior.
13. Fantastic and uninviting behavior, with drink and sometimes without.
14. Suicide rarely carried out.
15. Sex life impersonal, trivial and poorly integrated.
16. Failure to follow any life plan.[25]

Cleckley described the psychopath who is likely to end up in prison as easy to talk with, friendly, and frequently of superior intelligence. Perceptual reality is not distorted, prevailing social values may be accepted verbally, and excellent logical reasoning exists. The sociopath, who may have great verbal facility, is critical and even contrite about his former mistakes. He probably can foresee the consequences of his actions. These excellent rational powers, so apparent clinically and in hypothetical situations, do not carry over into behavior. Despite his surface rationality, the psychopath shows poor judgment in behavior and has a perplexing ability for creating situations in which no reasonable person would willingly participate. Furthermore, he suffers from specific loss of insight. He neither knows how others feel about him nor appreciates their perceptions. The sociopath is possibly equipped to gain insight, but he is unable to modify his behavior in the light of prior experience.

This baffling cognitive-behavioral paradox is seen in the sociopath's often motiveless antisocial behavior. He frequently commits crimes for small stakes and at great risk, yet he shows no evidence of being compulsive or neurotic. He is unable to formulate long-term goals and seems to be motivated to fail in life. He cannot be trusted in his accounts of the past, his statements of present intentions, or his promises for future conduct. He lies, seemingly without purpose, and with every appearance of sincerity, he manipulates the truth to gain his immediate ends.

The sociopath's untruthfulness is coupled with personal unreliability. He is grossly irresponsible, no matter how binding the obligation, in both trivial and serious matters. While the antisocial personality intermittently reveals convincing and conforming loyalty,[26] clinical or psychometric precision in predicting when he will be responsible, or when he will be violent, appears to be impossible. His behavior seems unrelated to mood, stress, or the amount at stake for himself or for others.

He appears to be unable to experience shame or remorse; usually he projects blame on others; and even his occasional blaming of himself seems hollow, casual, and instrumental. The sociopath is incapable of love and is unresponsive in interpersonal relations. While he may be attentive in small courtesies, and sometimes even obliging and generous, he cannot reciprocate kindness and trust. He is not usually motivated by altruistic concern, although he may claim to be. Nor can he express genuine emotions. In sum, the antisocial personality is impoverished in all aspects of affective reactions.

Cleckley also suggested that the sociopath is incapable of any deep personal commitment either to ideas or to persons. He often overindulges in sexual behavior, alcohol, drugs, and other "thrill-producing" activities. Sexual behavior is random, provoked frequently by whimlike impulses of little intensity, and it is devoid of emotional involvement.

Cleckley adopted the term "semantic disorder" or "semantic psychosis" to refer to this clinical picture. The sociopath mimics the human personality, and wears a "mask of sanity." Affective competencies are missing. The response to life is dissociated, and components of normal experience are not integrated into a wholly human reaction.

I have devoted considerable space to the Cleckley criteria since his *Mask of Sanity* has rekindled interest in the antisocial personality. These criteria have provided the basis of selection of subjects in many biomedical research studies beginning with the Schachter-Latane study, and including the work of Lykken, Hare, Ziskind, and the Goldman group. Most of these same criteria are also embedded in the MMPI psychopathic deviate (Pd) scale and in its many variations. And clinicians routinely cite this work in their own statements on dangerousness as indicated in chapter 5 in this volume.

Unfortunately, although Cleckley's list of symptoms caused a resurgence of interest in what was usually considered a clinical and research dead end, they cannot be operationalized. They are useless in the prediction of dangerousness or in elucidating the epidemiology, etiology, and treatment of violent and chronic miscreants.

Conceptions About Sociopathy

Defective Role-Taking

In a social psychological treatment of sociopathy, Gough contended that the sociological theory of role-playing accounts for the known facts about the antisocial personality, thereby offering hypotheses for empirical testing.[27] The antisocial personality, according to Gough, is pathologically deficient in role-taking ability. This deficiency is characterized by an inability to view the self as an object and to identify with another's point of view. Since other aspects of sociopathy are associated with this deficiency, Gough concluded that the causes of sociopathy must be sought in the causes of inadequacy in role-playing ability.

The role-taking deficit in the psychopath has been relatively neglected as a subject of research. There have been a few social-psychological studies. In practice, the defective role-taking hypothesis has been central to the development of I-level theory by Marguerite Warren.[28] In her system, delinquents are classified according to their level of maturity, I_1 being the most primitive and I_7, the most mature. In practice, juvenile correctional a few settings generally have mostly I_4 youth. Each category or I-level also has several subtypes, which makes classification even harder. The I-level classification system is still widely used to determine the placement and treatment of delinquents within institutional settings.

Warren's approach heavily draws on the seminal work of Piaget and more recently of Kohlberg, who have stipulated a stage-by-stage progression from moral immaturity to maturity. The analytic literature, as in the work of Erik Erikson, is also related to the role-taking view. The ideas of Laing are also closely allied to this conceptual framework.

The closest kinship, however, is with the symbolic interaction theory of Cooley and Mead in the sociological sphere. Cooley's "looking glass self" and Mead's I, me, and generalized other ideas are earlier versions of role-taking theory.

Intellectual kinship aside, the difficulty with this idea lies in understanding the etiology of defective role taking. The Gough CPI scale may measure it, as is also the case with two MMPI subscales and many other psychometric tests. But how and why one's growth to maturity is delayed or interrupted remains a mystery.

Albrecht and Sarbin,[29] arguing that antisocial sociopaths cannot take the time to put themselves in the role of the other before they act[30] and therefore are poor tension binders, hypothesized that such persons would be most responsive to annoying stimuli. Administering a 172-item annoyance question-naire to 60 male subjects (20 diagnosed as sociopaths, 27 diagnosed as neurotics, and 13 without psychiatric diagnosis), they found significant differences among groups on total means scores, with sociopaths having the highest, normals intermediate, and neurotics lowest mean annoyance scale scores.

McCord and McCord[31] offer another formulation of sociopathy and specify guiltlessness and lovelessness as the chief attributes of the antisocial person-ality.[32] These characteristics, it would appear, are considered basic to this syndrome; they are consistently employed in almost all contemporary uses of the concept.

The McCords attempted to evaluate the contributions of milieu therapy on young aggressive sociopathic boys at the Wiltwyck School in New York, wherein both individual and group therapy were combined in a warm, permissive environment. After painstaking study, the authors concluded that milieu therapy causes temporary alterations in the subjects' personality structures. Such an environment is easily manipulated by sociopaths, however; if the subjects had been followed after release, much of the optimism concerning successful treatment might have been dispelled by observing the behavior of sociopathic boys in a nonaccepting environment.

Sociological and Psychiatric Variables

In the most thorough sociological and psychiatric study of the antisocial sociopathic personality, Robins directed a ten-year research project representing a thirty-year retrospective study into the adult status of 524 child-guidance clinic patients of the St. Louis Municipal Psychiatric Clinic.[33] This patient group was predominantly comprised of male offspring of American-born Protestant parents of low socioeconomic status; blacks were excluded from the investiga-tion. Ninety percent of the subjects were located, 82 percent were interviewed, and 98 percent were successfully traced through adult records. On the basis of interview and record information, and for each of the nineteen areas of the subject's life in which he might have failed to conform to societal norms,[34] specific criteria for sociopathic behavior were established.[35] Using these criteria, two psychiatrists reviewed the sample and agreed on the mental condition of 80 percent of the subjects.[36] They were able to make specific diagnoses for 71 percent of the subjects. Robins, however, does not indicate the degree to which the 29 percent who could not be specifically diagnosed differed from those who were successfully diagnosed.[37]

The 94 St. Louis sociopathic subjects were compared with four other specific diagnostic groups that occurred frequently enough to permit statistical comparisons (anxiety neurosis, hysteria, schizophrenia, and alcoholism), and with a group of 100 control subjects from St. Louis, matched on race, area of residence, sex, age, and intelligence quotient.

This retrospective research project was concerned with three areas: distinctive symptoms of the sociopathic personality, a portrait of the adult sociopathic personality, and the predictability of later problems from childhood behavior. The findings in these three areas are complex, subject to differences in interpretation, and they were not analyzed or presented in very rigorous fashion.

Persons diagnosed as sociopathic personalities in the St. Louis study had more symptoms of social maladjustment than did any other diagnostic group; the three most common were financial dependence, poor work history, and multiple arrests. Four symptoms distinguished the sociopathic personality group at a statistically significant level from the comparison groups: poor marital history, impulsiveness, vagrancy, and the use of aliases.[38] The presence of one or more of the latter symptoms turned out to be among the best indicators of an antisocial personality diagnosis as an adult. Again, this is a circular argument since clincians are likely to use the same criteria in choosing the symptoms and making the diagnosis.

Thus the portrait of the St. Louis patient diagnosed as a sociopathic personality as an adult is contaminated by the use of the nineteen symptom areas that were used to diagnose subjects; the very criteria used for diagnosis were later treated as characteristics of the sociopath. However, four noncircular (that is, objectively assessed) aspects of sociopathy were also assessed: social adjustment, health, psychiatric symptoms, and treatment.

In general, persons diagnosed as sociopaths in the St. Louis study had a disproportionately high death rate, more than twice the national rate; felt themselves to be sicker than other groups; were extremely mobile; more often lived in the core city; were more often unemployed; had experienced long periods of unemployment; usually held low-ranking, blue-collar jobs; rarely held jobs for long; functioned longer in jobs in which they had little supervision; earned less when employed; were downwardly mobile in occupation; had low educational attainment; experienced little upward mobility from their fathers; were more frequently recipients of aid from public agencies; had the lowest percentage with established credit ratings; were more often divorced than any other group and less often currently living with spouse; tended to marry spouses with serious behavior problems; married somewhat younger than either patient or comparison groups; were slightly more often childless; were parents to children who were already showing marked emotional problems, few of whom graduated from high school; had the lowest rates of induction into the Armed Forces; were extreme medical and disciplinary problems in service; and served aborted periods of military service.

The St. Louis patients also had unusually high proportions of nontraffic arrests. Those arrested were arrested at least once for a major crime; had more convictions when arrested than all other subjects; were less likely to "burn out" in criminal behavior over time; had high rates of problem drinking; and were either currently experimenting with drugs (5 percent) or were or had been addicted to drugs (10 percent).

The sociopaths in the St. Louis study were also more often isolated from relatives and neighbors; belonged to very few formal organizations; had many neurotic and somatic symptoms; had rarely sought psychiatric care; had been hospitalized frequently in mental hospitals (21 percent); and had been more often previously diagnosed as sociopathic when hospitalized.

The preceding characteristics have been closely linked with lower social class status by sociologists, especially Matza,[39] Kahl,[40] and Komarovsky.[41] Social class may well be intervening to produce these marked differences and traits, although Robins made a concerted but somewhat ineffectual and unconvincing effort to contraindicate social class as an explanatory variable.[42]

Finally, as for childhood behaviors *predicting* sociopathy, Robins suggested that the Cleckley symptoms plus a history of status offenses were quite predictive of later problems.

Robins also noted that antisocial behavior by the patients' fathers was predictive of antisocial behavior for patients, particularly paternal desertion, arrest, excessive drinking, failure to support the family, and chronic unemployment. As for the effects of the family setting on sociopathic personality per se, however, Robins noted from the social and psychiatric histories that parental rejection does not appear to lead to sociopathy, and early separation from an antisocial father does not appear to prevent the development of sociopathy in the child. In the latter case, this may be due to the mother's lessened ability to exercise control over the child alone.

In conclusion, Robins suggested that a more precise study of the sociopathic personality could be made from a longitudinal study of consecutive births, thus minimizing the selectivity inherent in subjects volunteering or being forced to seek attention at mental health or child-guidance clinics. Such a study would be a difficult and expensive but potentially rewarding enterprise: psychiatric hypotheses and diagnoses could be tested against actual behavior.

Biological Substrates of Sociopathy

Despite the long-standing interest—particularly of European criminologists—in the biologic substrates of chronically antisocial behavior, few modern American criminologists have considered it appropriate to examine these aspects of criminal conduct. There are a variety of justifications for this neglect. Academic criminology in the United States is handled by departments of sociology rather than schools of law and medicine as in Europe and Latin America. Given their training and orientation, few sociologists are sympathetic to a biologic perspective. Instead, American criminology has been distinguished by its strong sociocultural emphasis and its view of criminal behavior as essentially learned and adaptive conduct. Another, and even more important, reason for this neglect of biologic investigation has been the sorry history of this perspective in the last hundred years. The extravagant claims, meager empirical evidence, naiveté, gross inadequacy, and stated or implied concepts of racial and ethnic inferiority in the work of the constitutionalists, the morphologists, the European traditionalists, and the early endocrinologists discredited the biological framework in the study of crime. Lombroso, Hooton, Sheldon, Burt, Lange, and others illustrate the problem: All argued some aspect of constitutional inferiority as the causal basis of criminal behavior; and all have been faulted on their research design, on their methodology, or on statistical grounds. Burt's classic, *The Young Delinquent*, and his work on the inheritance of intelligence, in particular, has been suspect on other grounds as well; in fact, Kamin claims that Cyril Burt's I.Q. research results were falsified.[43]

Also, biological variables and methodologies were ill adapted to social (macrolevel) phenomena until the 1960s or even later. Finally, American psychiatrists, at least those interested in criminology, have long held to a psychodynamic orientation that focuses on the psychogenic basis of intrapsychic and interpersonal pathologies rather than on a psychophysiologic basis. Given this intellectual climate and the disreputable history of biological theorizing, it is little wonder that criminologists have generally overlooked the very few important empirical biological observations.

Still, recent though limited studies of the antisocial sociopath have been conducted by physiological psychologists, biologists, and physicians, most of whom have focused on the physiological responses of the sociopath as distinguished from other prison inmates.

In 1949 Funkenstein, Greenblatt, and Solonion parenthetically mentioned the cardiovascular lability of chronically antisocial individuals.[44] Funkenstein, a psychiatrist, and his colleagues reported on fifteen sociopaths (thirteen men and two women) selected from a group of court referrals to the Boston Psychopathic Hospital. They characterized these subjects (twenty-one to thirty-nine years of age) as hostile recidivists. All had committed crimes of violence and exhibited no clinical signs of anxiety although they often claimed to be "nervous." Even though none of them volunteered any complaint of subjective discomfort, after an injection of 50 micrograms of epinephrine, thirteen of the fifteen sustained a systolic blood pressure rise of 75 mm Hg as compared to only nineteen of the eighty-five psychotic and neurotic patients and five of the fifteen controls.

In 1955 the psychologist D.T. Lykken reported on the performance of nineteen "primary" sociopath felons (twelve of whom were men) on eight assorted psychological tests.[45] On the two tests measuring autonomic function, the "primary" sociopaths produced a diminished galvanic skin response (GSR) to lying and a diminished conditionability of the GSR as compared with the noninstitutionalized controls. The first difference, the GSR to lying, approached the 0.05 level of significance. These differences were statistically different when the "primary" sociopaths were compared with a group of nineteen incarcerated "neurotic" sociopaths (i.e., the inmates who were labeled sociopathic by the prison staff but who did not meet Cleckley's clinical criteria).

In 1964 the social psychologists Schachter and Latane reported that fifteen imprisoned male sociopaths showed greater increases in pulse rate following an epinephrine injection than did fifteen inmate control subjects.[46] (Whether the controls of Schachter and Latane more closely related to Lykken's "neurotic" sociopaths or to his controls is unexplained.)

In 1965 the psychologist W.W. Lippert compared twenty-one "sociopathic" delinquents with twenty-one nonsociopathic delinquents and found that the "sociopaths" patterns of spontaneous GSR frequency were characterized by (1) lower resting levels, (2) lesser increases during experimental manipulation, (3) decreases to below resting levels following experimental manipulation, and (4) increased adaptation to repeated stimuli.[47]

In 1968 Hare, like Lippert, found that twenty-one primary psychopaths had higher skin resistance and less variability at rest than did twelve nonpsychopathic controls.[48] Furthermore, the psychopaths' GSR, cardiovascular, and orienting responses to mild stimuli, such as the solution of arithmetic problems, were less frequent than were the controls'.

Hakerem observed an exaggerated pupillary response in a group of patients who were later identified as "psychopaths."[49] This parenthetical observation was neither pursued nor published, however.

In the most recent and elegant assessment of the status of research in sociopathy, Hare underscores the assumption, now increasingly postulated, of a physiologic basis for this disorder.[50] Substantial emphasis has been placed on some prominent biological correlates of sociopathy, specifically:

1. The EEG patterns of some sociopaths resemble children's. This has led some investigators to the hypothesis of delayed maturation of some cortical neuronal mechanism.[51] These abnormal EEGs, often found in their parents as well, are characterized by a predominantly slow wave pattern, a pattern found in states of hypoarousal. See Goldman's discussion in the next chapter.

2. In some sociopaths, Hare argues that limbic system dysfunction, as evidenced in an abnormal slow wave EEG, seems to be involved.[52]

3. From this evidence, one may conclude that psychopathy may depend on a decreased state of cortical excitability and on an attenuation of sensory input.[53]

4. Some sociopaths display not only symptoms of hypoarousal but also of sensory deprivation. For example, it has been consistently observed that there is a paradoxical increase in aggressivity and other emotionality in certain sociopaths treated with drugs, such as barbiturates, neuroleptics, and ethanol—substances that usually promote sensory deprivation and passivity.[54]

5. Certain sociopaths demonstrate a pathological need for stimulation[55] and appear to be at a low end of an arousal continuum. One would expect from

these observations that some sociopaths would avoid the use of depressants. Robins indeed found this to be the case[56]; on the other hand, Hill found that depressants improve the behavior of *aggressive* sociopaths.[57]

6. Some sociopaths exhibit stereotyped behavior.[58] In view of poor space-time integration and stereotypical behavior, there is a likelihood that basal ganglia dysfunction may be involved.

7. Definite sexual differences in the median age of the onset of sociopathic symptoms may not be entirely socioculturally determined. Whereas in boys, symptoms may appear as early as seven years of age, they tend to occur later, around thirteen, in girls and to be less severe. There may be a sex-related difference in certain kinds of sociopathy together with a possible biological explanation as indicated in Robins's research.

8. Sociopaths seem to improve with age, thus supporting the concept of delayed maturation.[59] But only a certain type of sociopath will improve, while others will continue to demonstrate symptoms for life unless intervention is successful.

9. On the basis of the assumption that sociopathic behavior is somehow a consequence of hypoarousal, MacCulloch and Feldman suggested that stimulants such as amphetamine might have utility in the treatment of sociopaths.[60] However, Hare rightly adds social processing to chemotherapy as a potential means of management and growth to maturity.[61]

Heterogeneity of Sociopathy

Clearly, some of this research in sociopathy suggests a biological etiology, yet there has been little statistical validation of this hypothesis within and among studies conducted at different laboratories.[62] Explanations of this lack of replication may lie in the operational definitions of sociopathy, and the selection of different sociopathic types for experimental treatment.

After attempting to replicate the seminal work of Schachter and Latane in which a unique biological response was described in sociopaths, it became clear to our group that even the rigorous selection procedures we used did not yield a homogeneous group; marked variability in biologic and other measures made interpretation hazardous. We soon concluded that much of this variation, also noted by others, could be explained by the existence of at least two subgroups of antisocial personality types.

Our own multidisciplinary investigation, begun in 1965 at the Ohio Penitentiary and involving nineteen "primary" sociopaths, ten mixed, and fourteen nonsociopaths, as defined by a psychiatric evaluation, psychometrics (the Lykken, MMPI and Cleckley scales), and criminal history criteria (percentage of time spent in prisons, number of prior offenses) revealed that the "primary" sociopaths were not homogeneous with regard to such sociocultural variables as previous antisocial history, family characteristics, psychological profiles, and attitudes. As a result, using the Lykken scale scores as the criterion, the "primary" sociopaths were divided into two types, "hostile" and "simple." These types proved to be significantly different from each other on nearly all the sociocultural and psychological measures. Most important, only the "simple" (reasonably nonaggressive) sociopaths demonstrated the cardiac lability to epinephrine previously ascribed to sociopaths in general.[63]

The researchers concluded that the sociopath's autonomic responses demonstrated in characteristic overt behavior is paralleled by a characteristic physiologic behavior. Based on research at three Ohio prisons, the Goldman group hypothesized that a logical case could be made that both abnormal physiological and abnormal social behavior in the simple sociopath result from a single, simple, structural biological defect. Further, the most parsimonious lesion consistent with the available physiological data is simply a diminished function (partial or total) of the catecholamine-secreting nerve endings, including those involved with sensory receptors. Such a lesion would produce a deficit in processing emotion-laden stimuli and would yield the clinical picture that psychiatrists have long observed.

It is reasonable to assume that a defect already observed for three disparate effectors—heart, skin, and pupil—is general among catecholamine-secreting neurons. Since other evidence, both physiologic and anatomic, indicates that the sympathetic nervous system modulates sensory input at several levels, one result of such a general sympathetic nervous system defect would be a reduction in and distortion of incoming stimuli in the "simple" sociopath.[64] In point of fact, both Schoenherr[65] and Hare[66] have already demonstrated an elevated threshold for electric shock in sociopathic prisoners.

Two specific consequences may result from this nervous system defect in the catecholamine-secreting neurons. First, the lesion may cause the neurons to fail to develop normally (hence the ideas of "delayed maturation") and later "burn out," which has been observed clinically in the antisocial personality. Second, the significant neurons may develop normally but later regress or degenerate for reasons not now understood.

This biological model of sociopathy (there are competing models) calls attention to the superficial similarity between antisocial personality in the adult and hyperkinesis in the child. Like the Kraepelin nosology in psychiatry that makes sociopathy a residual disorder, hyperkinesis, for much the same reasons, has only recently been "discovered" to be a common disease in childhood which responds to pharmacologic intervention.[67]

With this parallel in mind it is conceivable and probable that defects in the nervous system could be compensated by medical means.[68] Perhaps medical treatment could be a preventive measure when applied prior to the onset of the disease, again as with hyperkinetic children. But in those in whom detection is delayed until the disorder has fully developed, the defect will have influenced behavior already; years of faulty programming would continue to determine behavior even after any original biologic basis had been removed or compensated. Hence even a medical solution to the sociopath's problem would be insufficient; if the assumptions of our team are correct, therapeutic intervention, of necessity, will have to include resocialization.

The issue is far from being resolved. We are still very much in ignorance of the course, mechanisms, and etiology of the behavior pattern and mental status currently called antisocial personality. Despite increased pharmacologic treatment of those designated as sociopaths, the chronically antisocial individual is likely to tax our ingenuity and patience in the foreseeable future to perhaps an even greater extent than he has in the past. In conclusion, there is considerable room for pessimism, notwithstanding the return of the medical and biological specialists to the field.

The next chapter, concerning the neurobiology of violence, suggests a variety of biological paradigms and the corresponding treatment approaches. The simplest way of concluding this chapter is to say that one solid hypothesis worth pursuing is that the psychopath, sociopath, or antisocial personality is a hyperkinetic child grown up. While many—indeed, probably most—of these children mature at puberty, some evidently do not. It is from this pool that the ever-present antisocial personalities may well be drawn. If so, there may yet be some hope for the future of these children and the troublesome adults they frequently become.

Notes

1. *The Diagnostic and Statistical Handbook of Mental Disorders*, American Psychiatric Association, 1952.

2. *The Diagnostic and Statistical Handbook of Mental Disorders*, American Psychiatric Association, 1968.

3. "Psychopathic personality" was the generic term used to refer to a large group of disorders that were regarded by many physicians and clinicians as diverse in nature, and as having too little in common to justify subsuming them under the general term. Furthermore, practitioners seldom used the term except to refer, not to the more heterogeneous group, but to only one of the disorders, psychopathy.

4. An excellent summary of these attributes may be found in Hervey Cleckley, "Psychopathic States," in S. Arieti (ed.), *American Handbook of Psychiatry* (New York: Basic Books, 1962), pp. 567-588. See also Alfred Noyes and I. Kolb, *Modern Clinical Psychiatry* (Philadelphia: Saunders, 1963), pp. 460-464; Eli Robins, "Personality Disorders; II: Sociopathic Types: Antisocial Disorders and Sexual Deviations," in A. Freeman and H. Kaplan (eds.),

Comprehensive Textbook of Psychiatry (Baltimore: Williams and Wilkins, 1967), pp. 955-956; and William McCord and Joan McCord, *Psychopathy and Delinquency* (New York: Grune and Stratton, 1956), pp. 47-81; Rudolph Kaelbling and Ralph M. Patterson, *Eclectic Psychiatry* (Springfield, Ill.: Charles Thomas, 1966), p. 371; Ian Gregory, *Psychiatry* (Philadelphia: Saunders, 1961), pp. 52-67.

5. Hervey Cleckley, *The Mask of Sanity* (St. Louis: Mosby, 1950), Appendix A. Bernard Glueck investigated 608 Sing Sing inmates, 18.9 percent of whom were found to be sociopaths; quoted in Sydney Maughs, "A Concept of Psychopathy and Psychopathic Personality: Its Evolution and Historical Development," *Journal of Criminal Psychopathology* 2 (April 1941): 480.

6. Lee N. Robins, *Deviant Children Grown Up* (Baltimore: Williams and Wilkins, 1966).

7. Fritz Redl and David Wineman, *Children Who Hate* (Glencoe, Ill.: Free Press, 1951).

8. Lewis Yablonsky, *The Violent Gang* (New York: Macmillan, 1962).

9. Such opinions are found in Robins, p. 2; Freedman and Kaplan, p. 958; Noyes and Kolb, pp. 464-465; Cleckley, pp. 585-587; and D.J. McCarthy and K.M. Corrin, *Medical Treatment of Mental Diseases* (Philadelphia: Lippincott, 1955), pp. 415-418.

10. Robert D. Hare, *Psychopathy: Theory and Research* (New York: Wiley, 1970), pp. 13-25.

11. Maughs, pp. 465-499.

12. Harry E. Allen, *Bio-social Correlates of Two Types of Anti-Social Sociopaths*, Ph.D. dissertation, Ohio State University, 1969.

13. Maughs, p. 329.

14. Raffele Garofalo, *Criminology* (Boston: Little, Brown, 1914), p. 80.

15. Cesare Lombroso, *Crime: Its Causes and Remedies* (Boston: Little, Brown, 1911).

16. Ibid., pp. 365-366.

17. Ibid., p. 423.

18. Maughs, p. 487.

19. Quoted in P.K. Henderson, *Psychopathic States* (New York: Norton, 1939), p. 27.

20. G.N. Thompson, "Psychopathy," *Archives of Criminal Psychodynamics* 4, no. 2 (Spring 1961): 736-749.

21. Henderson.

22. Harry Kozol, a more recent contributor, also related genius and sociopathy, and stated that the same dynamics operate in both. The level of

assault differs—the genius creates whereas the sociopath makes his attacks for "kicks," yet both are characterized by identical factors. There is dissociation between basic impulse patterns and the development of social pseudocon-formity. They learn to conform for their own benefit, but this educative process appears unrelated to the primitive impulse structure. This separation or pre-schizopathy accounts for the lack of internal control and the primitiveness of goals which characterizes them. Maughs, p. 484.

23. Henderson, pp. 128-129.

24. Hervey Cleckley, *Mask of Sanity*, 4th ed. (St. Louis: Mosby, 1964).

25. Ibid., pp. 363-400.

26. Kaelbling and Patterson, p. 372.

27. Harrison Gough, "A Sociological Theory of Psychopathy," *American Journal of Sociology* 53 (March 1948): 359-366; see also B. Baker, "Accuracy of Social Perceptions of Psychopathic and Non-Psychopathic Prison Inmates," unpublished manuscript, 1954, summarized in T.R. Sarbin, "Role Theory," in Gardner Lindzey (ed.), *Handbook of Social Psychology* (Cambridge, Mass.: Addison-Wesley, 1954), p. 246.

28. Marguerite Q. Warren, *The Community Treatment Project: An Integration of Theories of Causation and Correctional Practice*, California Youth Authority, Sacramento: May 14, 1965; and "Implications of a Typology of Delinquents for Measures of Behavior Change: A Plea for Complexity," *California Youth Authority Quarterly* 18, no. 3 (1965): 6-13.

29. R. Albrecht, and T.R. Sarbin, "Contributions to Role-taking Theory: Annoyability as a Function of the Self," unpublished manuscript, 1954; Lindzey, p. 246.

30. This point is basic to Gough's role-taking theory of sociopathy, following George H. Mead, *Mind, Self and Society* (Chicago: University of Chicago Press, 1934). See Gough, "A Sociological Theory of Psychopathy."

31. McCord and McCord.

32. Ibid., p. 2.

33. Robins, pp. 90-92.

34. The specific criteria are found in Robins, p. 80.

35. The median number of areas in which subjects given the diagnosis of antisocial sociopathic personality met the various criteria for failure to conform to societal norms was first reported to be eleven (p. 80). In the next paragraph it was reported that thirteen of the nineteen symptoms occurred in at least half the subjects who were diagnosed to have antisocial sociopathic personalities. Five pages later, Robins noted that 69 percent of the sociopathic group had at least nine of these nineteen symptoms.

36. The psychiatrists were aware that the topic of interest was antisocial sociopathic personality; a relatively high proportion (15.6 percent) were diag-

nosed sociopathic. It may well have been that "blind" evaluators would not have found such a high proportion to be sociopathic.

37. This introduces possible unknown biases into a study group that is not necessarily representative of any mentally disordered population.

38. Robins, p. 85.

39. David Matza, "Poverty and Disrepute," in Robert K. Merton and Robert Nisbet (eds.), *Contemporary Social Problems* (New York: Harcourt, Brace and World, 1966), pp. 619-669.

40. Joseph Kahl, *The American Class Structure* (New York: Rinehart, 1957), pp. 205-215.

41. Mirra Komarovsky, *Blue-Collar Marriage* (New York: Random House, 1964).

42. Robins's treatment of social class as a variable is at best less than ideal. Her study group is somewhat vaguely broken into "blue collar" and "white collar" on the basis of father's occupation; 24 percent of the former and 13 percent of the latter were found to be sociopathic. This represents a ratio of almost 2:1. It may be that sociopathy is concentrated in the lower class due to the relative breakdown in socialization, or due to the sociopath's having drifted downward. A third possibility is that psychiatrists see such antisocial behavior of the lower class as sociopathy, exhibiting middle-class perspective as professional judgment. Perhaps all three may be operating, although Robins argues against the last. However, the argument would have been stronger if she had presented the average number of symptoms necessary for diagnosis as sociopath for the lower and middle class, separately.

43. "IQ and Heredity: Suspicion of Fraud Beclouds Classic Experiment," News and Comment, *Science* (November 26, 1976) 194:916-919.

44. D.H. Funkenstein, M. Greenblatt, and H.C. Solonion, "Psychophysiological Study of Mentally Ill Patients," *American Journal of Psychiatry*, 106 (1949): 359-366.

45. D.T. Lykken, *A Study of Anxiety in the Sociopath Personality*, Ph.D. dissertation, University of Minnesota, Minneapolis (Ann Arbor: University Microfilms, 1955, no. 55-944).

46. Stanley Schachter and Bibb Latane, "Crime, Cognition and the Autonomic Nervous System," in David Levine (ed.), *Nebraska Symposium of Motivation* (Lincoln: University of Nebraska Press, 1964), pp. 271-274.

47. W.W. Lippert, *The Electrodermal System of the Sociopath*, Ph.D. dissertation, University of Cincinnati (Ann Arbor: University Microfilms, 1965, no. 65-12921).

48. R.D. Hare, "Psychopathy, Autonomic Functioning, and the Orienting Response." *Journal of Abnormal Psychology* 73, suppl. (1968): 1-24.

49. Gad Hakerem, personal communication, September 1968.

50. Hare, *Psychopathy*, p. 33.

51. L. Kiloh, and J.W. Osselton, *Clinical Electroencephalography* (Washington: Butterworth, 1966); D.B. Lindsley, "The Ontogeny of Pleasure: Neural and Behavioral Development," in R.G. Heath (ed.), *The Role of Pleasure in Behavior* (New York: Harper & Row, 1964), pp. 3-22; M.E. Scheibel and A.B. Scheibel, "Some Neural Substrates of Postnatal Development," in M. Hoffman and L. Hoffman (eds.), *Review of Child Development Research*, vol. 1 (New York: Russell Sage, 1954), pp. 481-519.

52. Hare, *Psychopathy*, pp. 30-36.

53. Ibid., p. 36; L.A. Lindner, H. Goldman, S. Dinitz, and H.E. Allen, "Antisocial Personality Type with Cardiac Lability," *Archives of General Psychiatry* 23 (1970): 260-267.

54. Harold Goldman, "Sociopathy and Diseases of Arousal," *Quaderni di Criminologia Clinica* 2 (1973): 175-194 (printed in 1975).

55. Herbert C. Quay, "Psychopathic Personality and Pathological Stimulation Seeking," *American Journal of Psychiatry* 122 (1965): 180-183; A. Petrie, *Individuality in Pain and Suffering* (Chicago: University of Chicago Press, 1967); H.J. Eysenck, *The Biological Basis of Personality* (Springfield, Ill.: Charles C. Thomas, 1967). See also Goldman, pp. 175-194.

56. Lee Robins, *Deviant Children Grow Up*. In an unpublished study Lindner, Goldman, Dinitz, Allen, and Schultz found that female sociopathic prisoners at the Ohio Reformatory for Women were peculiarly free of involvement with alcohol and barbiturates. They seemed to experience an adverse reaction from other depressants as well. See Christine Schultz, "Sociopathic and and Non-Sociopathic Female Felons," unpublished Ph.D. dissertation, Ohio State University, 1973.

57. D. Hill, "Amphetamine in Psychopathic States," *British Journal of Addiction* 44 (1947): 50-54.

58. Hare, *Psychopathy*, p. 89.

59. Eugene Ziskind, paper presented at "Workshop on Psychophysiological Responses in the Sociopath," New Orleans, La., November 1970.

60. M.J. MacCulloch, and M.P. Feldman, "Personality Structure and its Relation to Success in the Treatment of Homosexuals by Anticipatory Avoidance Conditioning," unpublished manuscript, cited in Hare, *Psychopathy*, p. 117.

61. Hare, *Psychopathy*, p. 118.

62. Helmut Schmidt, Donald Smeltzer, and Harold Goldman, "Antisocial Personality (Sociopathy) and Heart Rate Response to Epinephrine Infusion," paper presented to the American Association for the Advancement of Science, New Orleans, February 23, 1977.

63. Harry Allen, *Bio-social Correlates of Two Types of Antisocial Socio-*

paths, Ph.D. dissertation, Ohio State University (Ann Arbor: University Microfilms, 1969, no. 70-13971); H.E. Allen, L.A. Lindner, H. Goldman, and S. Dinitz, "The Social and Bio-medical Correlates of Sociopathy," *Criminologica* 6 (1969): 68-75; H.E. Allen, L.A. Lindner, H. Goldman, and S. Dinitz, "Hostile and Simple Sociopaths: An Empirical Typology," *Criminology* 9 (1971): 27-47; H. Goldman, L. Lindner, S. Dinitz, and H. Allen, "The Simple Sociopath: Physiologic and Sociologic Characteristics," *Biological Psychiatry* 3 (1971): 77-83; Lindner, Goldman, Dinitz, and Allen, "Antisocial Personality Type With Cardiac Lability"; Goldman, "Sociopathy and Diseases of Arousal."

64. E. Bulbring, "Biophysical Changes Produced by Adrenaline and Noradrenaline," in J.R. Vane, G.E.W. Volstenholme, and M. O'Connor (eds.), *Adrenergic Mechanisms* (Boston: Little, Brown, 1961), pp. 275-287; J.H. Burn, "The Relation of Adrenaline to Acetylcholine in the Nervous System," *Physiology Review* 25 (1945): 377-394; K.E. Chernetski, "Sympathetic Enhancement of Peripheral Sensory Input in the Frog," *Journal of Neurophysiology* 27 (1964): 493-515; E. Eldred, H.N. Schnitzlein, and J. Buchwald, "Response of Muscle Spindles to Stimulation of the Sympathetic Trunk," *Exp. Neurol.* 2 (1960): 187-195; W.R. Lowenstein, and R. Altimirano-Orrego, "Enhancement of Activity in a Paciniam Corpuscle by Sympathomimetic Agents," *Nature* 178 (1956): 1292-1293; L.M. Beidler, "Mechanisms of Gustatory and Olfactory Receptor Stimulation," in W.A. Rosenblith (ed.), *Sensory Communication* (New York: Wiley and MIT Press, 1961), pp. 294-307; A.P. Rodriguez-Perez, "On the Existence of Accessory Unmyelinated Fibers in the Meissher's Corpuscles of the Pulp of the Human Toe," *Dermatologica* 129 (1964): 468-474.

65. J. Schoenherr, *Avoidance of Noxious Stimulation in Psychopathic Personality*, Ph.D. dissertation, University of California at Los Angeles (Ann Arbor: University Microfilms, 1965, no. 64-8334).

66. R.D. Hare, "Detection Threshold for Electric Shock in Psychopaths," *Journal of Abnormal Psychology* 73 (1968): 268-272.

67. L.E. Arnold, V. Kirikcuk, S. Corson, and E. Corson, "Levoamphetamine and Dextro-amphetamine: Differential Effect on Aggression and Hyperkinesis in Children and Dogs," *American Journal of Psychiatry* 130 (1973): 165-170.

68. H. Allen, S. Dinitz, T. Foster, H. Goldman, and L. Lindner, "Sociopathy: An Experiment in Internal Environmental Control," *American Behavioral Scientist* 20 (1976): 215-226. In this article the authors describe an attempt to remedy the postulated defect in 41 prisoners through the use of imipramine (Tofranil). This experiment was aborted on the advice of counsel following the *Kaimowitz* v. *Michigan Department of Mental Health* and *Mackey* v. *Procunier* rulings in 1973. During the course of the double blind experiment, the sociopathic subjects seemed to benefit materially from the drug regimen while the nonsociopaths did not. See T.W. Foster, "Drug Therapy for Sociopathic

Offenders: An Experimental Treatment Program Utilizing Imipramine Hydro-
chloride," Ph.D. Dissertation, Ohio State University, 1975, for an intensive
discussion of this experiment and case history documents.

The Limits of Clockwork: The Neurobiology of Violent Behavior

Harold Goldman

In a mechanical age, we look to tinkers to solve our problems. Impatient with time as the healer, accustomed to the triumphs of science in eliminating diseases and transforming society, we hope that the laboratories will turn up a cure for violence. The hope is humane and pervasive. Psychiatrists and humanists look at the prison as an anachronism of misery beyond amelioration by architecture or enlightened administration. It survives principally because we do not know what else to do with the dangerous offenders whom we consign to its custody. It is plausible to prophesy, as both psychiatrists and humanists often do, that science will find a better way; dangerousness can be mended by the tinker.

But there is fear as well as hope. The power to make peaceful citizens out of bestial thugs, if it ever becomes available, will be new and vast. What can be done to the thug for good reasons can also be done to ordinary citizens for bad reasons. The twentieth century has seen hideous abuses of power, so it is natural to be apprehensive about the creation of new means to increase it.

Both hopes and fears die hard, and this chapter will show that neither can be laid to rest completely. However, any consideration of control and treatment of the dangerous offender must include what is known and conjectured about the biological sources of violent behavior. This survey will reveal the capability of helping a few kinds of violent offenders, the possibility of helping more, and the debris of many shattered beliefs and theories. Most violence will end only with the end of hatred and the myriad reasons for hatred. Nevertheless, it is true that some violence originates in twisted physiology, and it is here that the medical tinker can play an indispensable part in treating the nervous systems of men and women inflamed with rage beyond reason or hate.

For the last century, generations have drawn on biomedical knowledge for an understanding of violent behavior. The resulting interpretations of the origins of human violence have led to interventions that have generally demonstrated the limited usefulness of knowledge in this domain. Since the 1870s, dangerousness has been successively attributed to "atavism," hereditary defects, constitutional inferiority, gross endocrine malfunctions, and to various kinds of brain damage.

Each of these perspectives generated strategies for the treatment, management, and control of dangerous persons. "Atavistic" criminals were banished wherever banishment was practical. Then eugenicists prescribed the sterilization of mental and moral defectives, including the unfortunates classified as constitutional psychopathic inferiors. Fear of the Jukes and Kallikaks induced the United States Supreme Court to sanction surgical interventions to end the propagation of subhuman creatures unfit for participation in civilized life [47].

We are still in the process of emerging from a cultural preoccupation with the ranking of various classes of humanity on a scale ranging from Anglo-Saxon superiority to the irremediable inferiority of lesser breeds. Although we have discarded these concepts for the most part, many of the thought habits that they engendered continue to encumber us. We attribute undesirable behavior to constitutional defects for which compensation must be found if the individual is to function as a free agent in society. If the undesirable behavior consists of dangerousness to others, control must be instituted and maintained. The human condition is not that simple.

The paradigm that permitted scientists to view dangerousness as a disease has been abandoned, but the search for biological explanations of violence continues. As each concept is found wanting, it is replaced by new, if not necessarily more useful, conjectures. Examples abound; for example, the discovery of electrical activity in the brain and the identification of unique electrical patterns with convulsive disorders inspired interest in the electro-encephalographic profiles of overtly antisocial individuals. Peculiar patterns were found that were thought to be associated with retarded maturation of the nervous system. Far in advance of any practical use, institutions for the evaluation of abnormal persons built up libraries of electroencephalographic records, even though they still have no actual use in the administration of treatment.

More recently, eager specialists fastened on a tentative report that persons with the XYY chromosomal structure were given to aggressive, super-masculine behavior, often criminal in nature. Typically, such men are tall and have unusual skeletal conformations, thereby simplifying methodological problems in the study of the hypothesis generated by this report. The original study was cautious, and its subsequent interpretation was shown to be erroneous [178], but it is likely that genetic testing (karyotyping) of tall males will persist for years to come.

Dangerous behavior tends to provoke clinicians into the application of excessive remedies. The castration of sex offenders became a treatment of choice in some clinics without consideration of the possible effectiveness of less radical treatment. Forensic medicine is still haunted by the tragic consequences of the irresponsible legitimation of prefrontal lobotomies that, hardly twenty-five years ago, converted sentient human beings into barely animate objects. Of all people, scientists should know better than to expect the discovery of a philosopher's stone capable of transforming a person prone to violence into a reliably peaceful citizen, but the search proceeds. Even where sound theory has emerged, its application has been modest in its effects.

The scientific ledger in the biological study of violence consists mostly of now rejected hypotheses, some of them discredited at dismaying human cost. This discouraging experience commands us to be cautious in assessing the claims of the present generation of biologists. Nevertheless, some current conceptions are qualitatively different from previous biomedical approaches. Advancing technology, made possible by rapid progress in physics, biochemistry, optics, and other disciplines, has opened many hitherto inaccessible biologic subsystems for study. Empirical observation, using techniques undreamed of as recently as the fifties, can confirm biologists' speculations so that theories can be buttressed and systems built. In spite of past disillusionment, there is reason to believe that we now have more effective means to modify the mechanisms responsible for abnormal behavior. Our decisions, both legal and medical, need not depend so heavily on unconfirmed speculation.

Nevertheless, we must deflate the enthusiasm of some policy-makers who disregard the cautionary hedges surrounding a hopeful scientific message. The relatively successful treatments for some psychotic, hyperkinetic, and depressive disorders developed during the last twenty-five years have given rise to expectations that some character disorders will also yield to new developments in biology and medicine. Drawing on the advertising cliche, some commentators seem to believe that "the future is now." Hope may again exceed performance.

The psychic deformations that create the basis for violent acts against others are not attributable to processes that medical intervention can readily redirect. The current optimism of the biologist is based on the expectation that hostile and destructive men and women, from whatever cause, can be retrained with the benefit of relatively mild pharmacological interventions with reversible consequences and without unacceptable side effects. Few conditions will respond to a single remedy, and none of the remedies in sight is likely to be immediately effective. The gains ahead will be difficult to make, and it is not likely that their effects on individuals will be especially dramatic.

This chapter has two sections: The first contains an explication of certain models of the biological substrates of animal and human behaviors. This review will (1) outline the ways in which biologists link some forms of repetitively violent behavior to physiological abnormalities, and (2) discuss the strategies by which these abnormalities appear to be amenable to intervention.

The second section (1) covers the states of the therapies currently in use to modify conditions considered to be dangerous; (2) assesses the effectiveness of these methods as now practiced; and (3) describes some apparently promising emerging treatments, commenting on their feasibility for intervention with dangerous persons.

The Biology of Violence

In spite of its unpalatable implications, it is a fundamental element in any paradigm for research in the neurobiology of violence that man is an animal whose conduct is determined by biological variables. It follows that his behavior has structural and functional origins, that components of the nervous system interact to formulate responses to the environment. The body may be considered to be in constant dialogue with persons and things in the environment, but this dialogue is conducted in an internal operating language through the nervous and endocrine systems. Experience is translated into this biological language, and the emotions constitute the organism's response to this experiential input, also couched in the language of the body's physical systems. Many of the mechanisms through which these systems interact are now accessible for study and, in the laboratory, can be modified by techniques applied to animal subjects. Violent, aggressive behavior in people has a counterpart in animals [24]. As perceived in the laboratory, intervention with animals offers a basis for intervention with man [146].

Although there is no consensus about linking morphologic and physiologic substrates to the expression of abnormal aggressive behavior, biologists generally agree that such derangements involve, in some way, structures in the anterior portion of the brain. The functions of these parts of the brain appear to be concerned with goal-directed behavior and the motivational and emotional concomitants associated with such behavior. Both the external stimulation of sensory systems and internal activity of the cerebral cortex and less well understood neural structures can evoke the integrated responses of visceral and somatic systems that characterize the physiological expression of aggressive behavior [49]. Much of what is known about the physiology of violence involves a group of interconnected brain structures (the limbic system); the functional significance of this system was recognized in the 1930s by Papez [119].

The Physiology of Violence: The Limbic System

Man appears to have inherited three brains (figure 4-1): an old, basically reptilian brain; a second inherited from lower mammals (paleomammalian); and the newest brain, a most recent development, that gives him his unique power of symbolic language (neomammalian) [91].

The primitive reptilian brain corresponds to the greater part of the human brain stem and contains much of the so-called recticular system, the hypothalamus, the midbrain, and the basal ganglia. It is filled with ancestral lore and memories that organize behavior in a predictable, often stereotyped, way as if it were programmed by an ancestral imprint.

The paleomammalian brain, built atop the reptilian brain, provides the organism with some release from its ancestral imprint by playing a fundamental role in emotional, aggressive, and sexual behavior. This more recent brain allows more freedom than the reptilian brain for learning and decision-making, and it permits both internal and external expression of emotions. In the evolution of

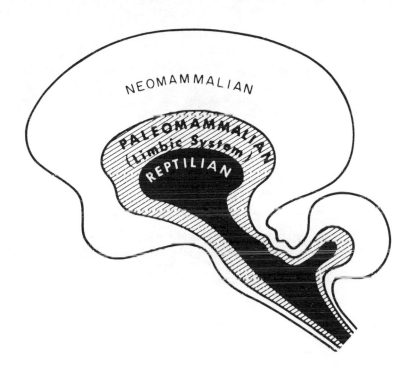

Source: "The Brain in Relation to Empathy and Medical Education," *Journal of Nervous and Mental Disorders* 144 (1967): 374-382. ©1967 The Williams and Wilkins Co., Baltimore. Reprinted by permission.

Figure 4-1. Hierarchical Organization of Three Basic Brain Types.

mammals, the distinctive feature of this brain is the appearance of a cortex with well-differentiated layers, ballooning out from the brain stem and covering the cerebral hemispheres. This primitive cortex and its related structures in the brain stem form the paleomammalian brain, providing the animal with a combined picture of the outside and inside world. Hence it is often referred to in the literature as the visceral or emotional brain. More descriptively, however, it is referred to simply as the limbic system because most of this old cortex is contained in the large limbic lobe, which surrounds the brain stem [89]. ("Limbic" means "forming a ring or border".) The limbic lobe is present in all species of mammals and organizes vegetative behaviors as well as certain "affects" in all mammals. It seems to operate at an animalistic level in both animal and man [e.g., 8, 21, 88, 89, 119, 171].

MacLean's scheme for limbic system organization (figure 4-2) omits the "new"—that is, the recently acquired cortex of higher mammals—and shows only the limbic lobe and its connection with the brain stem. The median forebrain

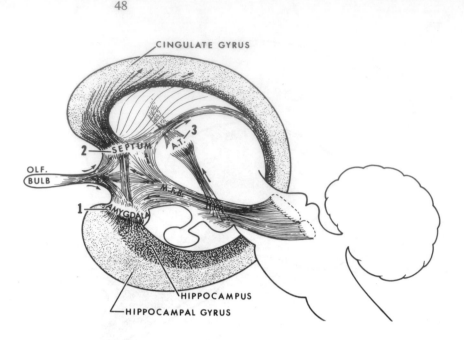

Source: "The Brain in Relation to Empathy and Medical Education," *Journal of Nervous and Mental Disorders* 144 (1967): 91. ©1967 The Williams and Wilkins Co., Baltimore. Repritned by permission.

Figure 4-2. The Limbic System Organization.

bundle is the major line of communication for neural traffic going back and forth between the limbic lobe, intermediate structures such as the hypothalamus and important cell stations in the brain stem. From the behavioral and neuroendocrine standpoint, it is important to recognize that the limbic cortex, in contrast to the neomammalian cortex, has many connections with the hypothalamus. The hypothalamus plays a major role in integrating the performance of primitive brain mechanisms involved in the survival of both the species and the individual: among these mechanisms are the physiological bases for the expression of emotion. In the human, the extensive enlargement of the neocortical mantle surrounding the limbic structures is responsible for much of the unique power to process symbols. However, people have *not* lost their dependence on the limbic system for the expression of emotional behavior [2, 17, 28, 34, 158]. In recent years several advances have been made in understanding the function of the low part of the limbic ring, which receives information from the amygdala. This region appears to be concerned with feeding functions and with behavior involved in the struggle to search out and obtain food—in short, with survival of the individual.

The portion of the cortex associated with the limbic system is especially susceptible to injury, circulatory insufficiency, and infectious processes. Damage to this region in humans often results in epileptic discharges that produce the same effects as stimulation of this region in animals. These effects include the feelings of hunger, thirst, nausea, suffocation, choking, retching, cold and warmth, and the need to defecate or urinate. There are also feelings of terror, fear, sadness, foreboding, strangeness, unreality, wanting to be alone, and persecution. The automatic behaviors that usually follow the aura of an epileptic seizure often appear to be an acting out of the subjective state, that is, eating, drinking, vomiting, manifesting anger, running, and screaming as if afraid.

Removal of lower parts of the limbic ring often gives a picture that is the reverse of that seen with stimulation. Surgical removal of large portions of structures in the lower half of the ring interferes with mechanisms essential for the individual's feeding and survival. After such surgery, animals such as monkeys or cats become tame and docile and repeatedly expose themselves to painful or harmful situations.

The functions of the lower part of the ring are balanced against those of the upper part, i.e., the individual's survival is often balanced against the survival of the species. Loss of the function of one part of the ring, therefore, is often associated with an increased display of the activities of the other part. Thus along with the tameness and docility after surgical damage of the lower part of the ring, animals display marked increase in sexual activity and sometimes rather bizarre sexual behavior. In human pathology cases have been reported in which irritative lesions involving the upper portion of the ring have resulted in strong, episodic sexual feelings. Stimulation of structures in the upper portion of the ring, therefore, leads to various sexual displays and, in man, to pleasurable feelings [53, 76, 115]. Observations such as these suggest that the upper part of the ring is partly concerned with elaborating pleasurable sexual affects.

There is a growing accumulation of experimental evidence both in animals and humans that correlates aggressive behavior with gross structural lesions in parts of the limbic system [8, 9, 44, 72, 88, 92, 93, 94, 95, 113, 114, 118, 119, 120, 152]. This evidence, for example, establishes that lesions in the hypothalamus of animals predictably induce the symptoms of rage. In humans, lesions in the hypothalamus have been documented in the progressive development of uncontrollable rage behavior [3]. Post-mortem examination of one such patient revealed a cyst that distorted the hypothalamus, thereby causing its atrophy. From another cruel experiment of nature, von Economo, in describing the consequences of an epidemic of encephalitis in 1917, drew attention to the relationship between somnolence and the destruction of the posterior hypothalamic region. He also described lesions in the anterior portion of the hypothalamus and related these to aggression and the "hyperkinetic" state [170]. Lesions in the hypothalamic area that are associated with aggressive behavior and rage reactions are produced mostly by tumors, but they may include vascular and traumatic damage as well. Some forty years ago, however, Papez [119] recognized that the intense emotional symptoms seen in rabies was related to a lesion in the hippocampus (figure 4-2), another region associated with the limbic system; he suggested that this was a clue to yet another "location" of emotional mechanisms. It is now clear that aggressive behavior and various symptoms of rage can be elicited by lesions in various places throughout the entire limbic system, and thus include areas from the anterior temporal lobe to the hippocampal formation, amygdala, and regions of the hypothalamus [4, 46]. Given the degree of interconnection, it is not unexpected that a lesion in one part of a complicated integrated system is apt to trigger activity in the other parts. It is difficult, therefore, to make inferences about causal relationships between structural changes in the limbic system or its associated structures and aggressive behavior, even though much is known about the effects of stimulation and ablation of subunits in this system.

Routine post-mortem examinations on individuals with persistently criminally aggressive behavior patterns have yielded little information other than to document that the incidence of gross lesions in the hippocampal-limbic system are rare. If abnormalities have been structural, then the lesions were too small to be detected by currently available methods. On the other hand, defects at a functional level have been suggested by frequent abnormal electroencepholographic (EEG) patterns in numbers of such violent persons.

Since much of the communication within the nervous system is electrical, the measurement of the EEG has become popular with many diagnosticians as a sensitive mirror of the cerebral functions of dangerous criminal offenders. Abnormalities in EEG activities have been attributed to criminal impulsivity [153], especially in murderers judged to be "insane" even when no epileptiform abnormalities are evident [142]. A number of EEG studies [60, 61, 176] have shown a high percentage of electrical abnormalities in so-called sociopathic individuals. The type of unusual electrical activity is not specific for this character disorder. In general, the incidence of EEG abnormalities in sociopathic groups is higher than that of psychoneurotic or schizophrenic populations. Despite the promise and the many thousands of such measurements, however, little information consistently or directly correlates EEG abnormalities with violence and aggression.

Ordinarily, the EEG reflects electrical activity chiefly in the cortex. In man, the measurement of electrical activity in structures deeper within the brain, unfortunately, has been performed only in a limited number of disease states largely determined by diagnostic requirements leading to surgical intervention, i.e., in cases of tumors and cerebrovascular accidents. On the other hand, the stimulation and recording of electrical activity deep within the brain in relation to aggressive behavior is well studied in other animals. There is a great deal of agreement in the data relating the brain's electrical activity with aggressive behavior in different species, particularly the rat, cat, and monkey. Although differences exist among species, the likelihood remains that the conclusions about animals may be pertinent for humans. *Generalization from experience with animals to the human condition should be done with great care, however.* Up to now, experiments with rats, cats, dogs, and monkeys have increased understanding, but they have had few important consequences for the treatment of the conditions we are considering here.

The Physiology of Violence: The Hypothalamus and Rage

Several portions of the brain, including the neocortex, the limbic cortex, and amygdala, appear to suppress primitive brain stem functions, particularly those concerned with the expression of anger [10]. Since some of their actions seem to be exerted at the level of the hypothalamus, surgical removal of these connections with the hypothalamus results in periodic fits of rage behavior in animals. There are intervening quiet periods during which seemingly innocuous stimuli produce an emotional display of savage behavior with somatic and visceral components similar to what intact cats display when they are attacked or attacking. This "sham" rage can also be elicited by stimulating certain limited regions of the brain stem and the forebrain [8, 21, 22, 32, 51, 55, 56, 57, 58, 59, 69, 100, 101, 125, 126, 139, 182].

In intact cats, stimulating the hypothalamus causes a display of rage, which is sometimes accompanied by an attack on nearby animals [136, 162] and even on the experimenter [58, 59, 65]. Similar kinds of behavior have been triggered by stimulating the hypothalamus in the opossum [137] and in the rat [181].

In summary, the neural structures within the brain involved in these aggressive reactions appear to be functionally and anatomically interrelated. The hypothalamus appears to be central to the development of antagonistic behavioral patterns; its destruction disrupts the expression of aggressive behavior. The amygdala influences aggressive behavior principally by modulating the activity of the hypothalamus, while the septum appears to inhibit the contributions of both the amygdala and hypothalamus to aggressive behavior. The midbrain serves mainly to relay information descending from higher structures but seems to possess some integrative capabilities as well. Though most of the large body of information about the nervous substrates of violent behavior is derived from species other than the human species, it may be pertinent to man nevertheless. Because so much of the structure and function of more primitive brains is replicated in humans, the physiologic viewpoints discussed in this section have formed the bases for most of the psychosurgical treatments of intractably aggressive individuals. These are discussed later.

Neurochemical Views on Aggressive Behaviors: Neurotransmitters

Violent behaviors, characterized in animals as affective aggression and predatory aggression [42, 128] differ in their modes of expression, the provoking stimuli, the neuroanatomical substrates, and their neurochemical modulation. Affective aggression has been the most extensively studied type of aggression; in the cat the prototype of this form of behavior has been called sham-rage [8], defense reaction [1], and affective attack behavior [57]. Such behavior may be evoked by lesions [8, 130], by stimulation [42, 52, 57, 133, 171], or by infliction of a painful stimulus [66, 164]. Affective aggression is characterized internally by intense and patterned activation of the visceral nervous system, resulting in symptoms of increased cardiac output, blood pressure, pupillary dilation, and so forth. Externally, it also involves a threatening or defensive posture, sometimes accompanied by vocalization. By contrast, predatory aggression elicits very little activity in the visceral nervous system and external displays include the swift, low mutilation killing of a natural prey, without much vocalization [74, 117, 171].

It is likely that two different neuronal pathways modulate these two forms of aggression. The pathway regulating affective aggression appears to be widely distributed, extending from the brain stem through the hypothalamus to the amygdala [39, 68]. These neural networks that organize attack behavior are themselves modulated by chemically specific neuronal arousal mechanisms that thereby inhibit or facilitate the display of affective behavior. In recent years, biological science has drawn on its increased capability for subcellular and molecular research. The study of aggressive behavior has benefited from this trend with the addition of new neurochemical insights to the older physiological information. Thus affective and predatory aggression not only have different neuroanatomical bases, but they may also have different neurochemical bases [128]. For a schematic presentation of the relationship between the neurotransmitters (to be discussed in this section), and predatory and affective aggression, see table 4-1.

A great deal of the neurochemistry of aggression focuses on the events at the junctions between nerves (synapses), for it is here that electrical communication is transduced to specific, secreted chemical information—neurotransmitters. Here also are exerted the actions of the many neuropharmacological agents that mimic or antagonize the actions of neurotransmitters. All available evidence suggests that neurons that secrete relatively simple neurotransmitter substances, norepinephrine (NE), acetylcholine (ACh), and serotonin (5-HT) modulate systems that organize each type of aggressive behavior in unique ways.

Norepinephrine, more than any other neurotransmitter [127], facilitates affective aggression and inhibits the expression of predatory aggression. NE metabolism is increased in the brains of animals in which affective aggression has been induced [16, 73, 81, 166, 173, 174]. Furthermore, drugs that facilitate NE's actions in the brain sometimes initiate or exacerbate aggressive behavior [33, 36, 37, 52, 79, 80, 85, 87, 123, 124, 129, 130, 132, 143, 144, 174, 182, 189]. Additionally, the release of NE in the brain appears to be proportional to the intensity of the evoked aggressive behavior [131].

Table 4-1
Different Actions of Some Central Neurotransmitters on Two Classes of Aggression

Neurotransmitter	Class of Aggression	
	Affective	Predatory
Norepinephrine (NE)	↑↑	↓
Acetylcholine (ACh)	↑	↑↑
Serotonin (5-HT)	↓	↓

In contrast to the action of brain NE mechanisms in affective aggression, NE appears to inhibit predatory aggression [64, 78, 116, 140], for reasons that are not yet clear.

In addition to noradrenergic neurons, (acetyl)cholinergic mechanisms help organize affective aggression. ACh, or drugs mimicking ACh, administered into the cerebral ventricles evoke a display of angry behavior and affective attack [11, 54, 90, 111]. This suggests that regions of the brain sensitive to ACh lie near the walls of the ventricles. Although ACh can trigger affective attack behavior, the most compelling evidence for the participation of cholinergic systems in aggression is in the regulation of predatory aggression [7, 151] rather than affective aggression. Using predatory frog- or mouse-killing behavior in rats as a model, local microinjections of ACh into specific sites in the hypothalamus and some associated regions can elicit a stereotyped killing response. On the other hand, microinjection of drugs, such as atropine, that antagonize the actions of ACh inhibit predatory killing by such "killer" rats. Such findings suggest that the natural release of the neurotransmitter ACh from cholinergic nerves facilitates predatory killing.

By contrast, recent evidence suggests that activities of neurons that secrete the neurotransmitter serotonin (5-HT) are preponderantly inhibitory to several modes of aggressive behavior. Drugs that block the synthesis of 5-HT facilitate both affective and predatory aggression [26, 38, 147, 148, 149, 159]. The successful treatment of affective disorders by means of lithium, which may act by increasing the availability of 5-HT in various brain regions, has led to speculations that aggressive behavior in both rats and people [150, 172] also can be controlled by similar substances. Thus various drugs that alter the production or actions of 5-HT—or, for that matter, NE—have been proposed in the treatment of affective aggression.

Obviously, no single neurotransmitter uniquely organizes either class of aggression; a number of other neurotransmitters probably interact in their expression. Moreover, the behavioral actions of various neurotransmitters is not uniquely limited to aggression; these agents obviously participate in other behaviors. The functions of these neurotransmitters, particularly NE and 5-HT, appear to be related to the modulation of a variety of organized behavior patterns. In view of the numbers of neurotransmitters participating in various aggressive behaviors, it is unlikely that interference with the action of one transmitter would control all types of aggressive behavior. For this reason, it is unlikely that any single drug would have a selective action on aggression without affecting other behaviors.

The implications for treatment of any chemically mediated behavior are scientifically far-reaching. The neurochemical paradigm focuses on portions of nervous control systems that are especially vulnerable to chemical modification both from within and outside the organism. These areas are both focuses for disease and targets for treatment. The paradigm expounded many years ago by Ralph W. Gerard, founder and past president of the Society for Neuroscience, that a "twisted molecule" was responsible for a "twisted thought" strongly suggests the ways behavior is and can be modified by molecules. Unlike most neurosurgical interventions, chemical interventions are likely to be reversible, less dangerous, and more readily accepted as well as abused.

Neurochemical Views on Aggressive Behaviors: Hormones

The relationship between hormones and aggressive behavior is an expansion of the view that endogenous chemical substances profoundly affect the functions of the nervous system. While neurotransmitters are secreted by nerves connected to specific structures, hormones—which also convey chemical messages—are secreted by specialized glands into the general blood circulation. As a consequence, these substances act more diffusely by affecting cells *throughout the body*, including those in the nervous system. Until recently, studies of the relationships between hormones and aggressive behavior has been limited mostly to the actions of sex steroids in animals rather than man.

In the area of steroidal regulation of aggression, two prejudices predominate. On the one hand, androgenic steroids, such as testosterone, may facilitate fighting behavior. On the other hand, estrogenic steroids may inhibit the expression of aggressive behavior. Thus males, who primarily secrete androgens, tend to be more aggressive than females, in whom estrogens are the preponderant sex steroid. Often, however, androgen manipulation in animals, whether by castration or injection, has led to conflicting results. Some investigators have reported diminished fighting behavior after castration and restored fighting after androgen replacement in mice [13], but the results have not always been consistent. For example, responses to androgens are also modified by strain and genetic factors [5, 43, 45], past experience [163], testing procedures [14], length of treatment [14], and drug potency [15]. On the other hand, estrogens, which do not affect development of aggressive behavior in very young mice, can inhibit fighting in mature males [157, 160].

Nonsexual behavior, such as the expression of aggressive behavior, is also sexually dimorphic and considered to be largely determined by hormonal action on both the developing, as well as the adult, nervous systems. Testosterone treatment of infant female mice leads to increased fighting behavior in the adult that is similar to the behavior of normal males and not characteristic of females [84, 160]. Conversely, neonatally castrated male rats fail to show typical male patterns of fighting even when treated as adults with androgens [25]. But when such animals are given replacement therapy in infancy with androgens, they display the same fighting behavior as that of normal animals when they become adults.

Androgens are related in some way also to the nervous mechanisms that organize rank and other social behaviors. For example, the behavior state in rhesus monkeys influences the level of testosterone in the blood with the opportunity for dominance increasing the level of the hormone, and an imposed social defeat situation lowering the hormonal level [138, 145].

Steroidal effects in humans and other primates are more complex. The secretion rate of testosterone in young men correlates well with the level of overt hostility. In older men, however, there is no correlation, nor is there a correlation between secretion rate and hostility in psychiatric patients [121]. In a recent study [77] the correlation of plasma testosterone with aggressive behavior in male prisoners was poor with respect to fighting in prison or with various psychological tests designed to assess aggressiveness. Elevated testosterone levels did correlate with a history of more violent crimes in adolescence, however, particularly with assault and attempted murder.

In contrast to androgens, female sex hormones generally reduce aggression in animals. Estradiol suppresses fighting in birds [29] and lizards [35]. In mammals the responses again are more complex. For example, estradiol in rhesus monkeys [102, 104] affects the frequency of patterns of aggressive behavior related to sexual activities. The synthetic estrogen, diethylstilbesterol, may eliminate excessive sexual activity and decrease "antisocial" behavior [31]. Medroxyprogesterone acetate tends to make sexually hyperactive boys more "tractable" [86] and in some aggressive men, treatment with medroxyprogesterone decreases aggression [105].

Bremer found that castration in men did not inhibit aggression nor affect their adjustment, except in relation to sex drive [18]. Furthermore, the treatment was not effective when the indications were merely excitement and impulsiveness.

In women, the endocrine relationship to behavior is never more obvious than in the premenstrual distress syndrome. Symptoms can vary from minor irritability to homicidal violence or severe depression; most aggressive and antisocial acting-out occurs during this time [107]. Among female prisoners, the majority of offenses requiring institutional segregation are committed just prior to menstruation, a time of relatively low circulating estrogen.

Other hormones or hormone-like substances may be directly or indirectly involved with violent behavior. Some of their disparate actions in the nervous system have been subjects of intensive study only recently. Thus there are relatively simple molecules made by parts of the brain or organs located near the brain, such as the pituitary glands, that affect several aspects of learning such as motivation, acquisition, retrieval, extinction, and arousal states [70], as well as the perception of pain. This class of substances may figure in the experimental generation of violence behavior (γ-endorphin, β-lipotropin 61-77-Guillemin[a]) and in its reversal as well.

This new class of regular substances consists of chains of relatively few amino acids called polypeptides. The polypeptides most intensively studied are those normally secreted by the pituitary glands, the adrenocorticotrophic hormone (ACTH), the melanocyte-stimulating hormone (MSH), and the anti-diuretic hormone (ADH) as well as fragments of these hormones. As the names imply, each has some easily characterized regulatory action on peripheral organs. In addition, however, it appears that these substances are carried in the blood, and that they exert profound effects on various behavioral mechanisms. Thus in animals, several of these substances that are secreted during stressful situations (i.e., fright, flight, or fight), by acting back on the brain independently of their other actions, can facilitate learning, focusing of attention, and retaining and retrieving learned responses. There are still relatively few studies on the effects of these peptides in humans, but there are indications that they act in the same way [103, 141]. The effects of fragments of these hormones, often polypeptides of no more than five amino acids, as well as more potent synthetic analogs, are being vigorously investigated in humans, particularly in the areas of amnesia and learning disabilities.

The growing list of other relatively simple endogenous substances that can alter arousal states [71, 122, 167], modify perceptions of pain [48], and affect attention, recall, and other aspects of learning have immediate medical utility. Furthermore, their recent discovery has already reshaped the way we think about the biologic substrates of normal and abnormal behavior. Substances of this nature, produced normally in the body and now easily synthesized in the laboratory, seem to be essential for the translation of experiential input into the biologic codes with which our brains organize the business of living. Body functions that produce or respond to these substances are newly recognized not only as possible sources of pathologic behavior but as points that are accessible to current biochemical and medical intervention, as well. So far there has been little discussion, publicly at least, of the possibility of using the agents to improve, for example, the memories of normal people, but "it is an idea that cannot help but occur to anyone who has ever forgotten anything" [98, 99]. There is also the far-reaching possibility of such substances being used to facilitate learning and conditioning programs, programs that can be designed not

---

[a]Reported at the 10th International Congress of Biochemistry, Hamburg, Germany, 1976.

only to treat behaviors of deficient or retarded individuals but of "oranges" whose "clockworks" produce socially unacceptable behavior. That this may be accomplished or abused with relative ease by mimicking normal endogenous processes that are reversible and nontoxic is awesome and ominous.

Traditional Biomedical Interventions

Each biomedical view presented so far has dealt with a different aspect of the way the nervous system handles and mishandles information, that is, how it receives it, translates it, stores it, and reacts to it. As might be expected, each of these paradigms has generated unique medical treatments that have included therapies based on psychological, psychophysiologic, neurosurgical, and psychopharmacological tools.

Although each treatment has usually evolved from an initial model in which a clear or possible medical problem was associated with aggressive behavior, treatments have gradually been extended to include individuals in which etiologies are unclear or unknown. For example, as more is learned about the interrelationships of parts of the brain in emotional expressions, the easier it has become to rationalize the interruption of such expressions even in the absence of a medical reason such as epilepsy. Sometimes unsubstantiated "subcortical epilepsy" is invoked as a reason for certain acting-out behavior and may become the basis for surgical or pharmacologic intervention.

The Anatomical Paradigm and Its Consequences
in Intervention

The belief in anatomical bases of mental illness has encouraged the exploration of surgical intervention for relief. Many neurosurgeons have performed substantial surgical treatments for patients suffering from severe psychiatric or neurological illnesses who also display intractable violence and aggression. Improved knowledge of the interrelationships of parts of the limbic system discussed earlier in the expression of aggressive behavior initially led to the extensive use of the extirpation or interruption of tracts to the frontal cortex. Subsequently, as techniques were refined, and in attempts to reduce morbidity, mortality, and unwanted interference with other behavior, neurosurgical treatments have become much more selective and discrete: They have come to involve specific regions of the amygdala, hypothalamus, thalamus, and cingulate portions of the cerebral cortex. There are thousands of amygdalotomies reported throughout the world for the treatment of a variety of clinical indications, all of which included violent or aggressive symptoms. Somewhat fewer hypothalotomies have been performed, again for similar reasons, with a marked calming effect reported in most patients. Similarly, surgical destruction of parts of the thalamus or cingulate cortex has been performed in patients suffering from a variety of illnesses including aggressive behavior; results have been mixed.

The success of early work with animals—e.g., stimulation experiments in cats [57] and monkeys [63] suggesting a hypothalamic component to the expression of aggression, or the ablation of prefrontal areas in chimpanzees as a cure for temper tantrums [67]—led to psychosurgery in human patients. Success with psychosurgery was sufficient to merit a Nobel Prize in 1949 for Moniz [106]. This same year marked a peak in the wave of psychosurgery that followed World War II. It is estimated that as many as 50,000 lobotomies were performed in the United States before they became less fashionable [27]. As methods of lesioning have become more precise, employing stereotaxic machines for accurate lesion placements, a high rate of surgical intervention continued; as many as 12,000 were performed from 1965 to 1968. The goals of such intervention were numerous: often to reduce otherwise intractable pain, tremor, spasticity, and seizures, but also to reduce emotional disturbances including aggression, hyperkinesis, and psychosis.

In 1951 Narabayashi [112] reported some success in the treatment of aggressive, assaultive patients with temporal lobe epilepsy by surgery in the amygdala. Eventually, such surgery was performed in the absence of temporal lobe epilepsy with only abnormal EEG and behavior disturbances as the criteria. By 1963 psychosurgery was employed additionally in mentally defective subjects to ameliorate hyperative or destructive conduct.

Although psychosurgery is not a casual undertaking, many thousands of severely troubled and troublesome patients were ultimately managed by psychosurgery during the fifties and sixties. Even now, many responsible neurosurgeons believe that to withhold such therapy from individuals with otherwise uncontrollably violent and aggressive behavior is to deprive them of their only significant chance for assistance and relief [49]. Insofar as behavior modification is concerned, however, evaluation of the outcomes of such surgical procedures has been equivocal. Moreover, there are the major problems of systematically researching and evaluating such subjects. In the past, crude surgical extirpation and major tractotomy in the central nervous system produced relatively gross personality changes in individuals. Of course, the treatments were also irreversible and very dangerous physically as well as behaviorally. More elegant, precisely located lesions have produced less general brain damage (lesions on the order of 1 millimeter in diameter).

Nevertheless, even though lesions are used to treat difficult behavioral problems, the consequences of lesions—even those of very circumscribed lesions—of highly interconnected structures in the brain proved to be global rather than specific on selected behavior patterns.

Most of the surgical procedures reported in the literature are described as successful, but many unreported attempts were probably less than successful.

Furthermore, estimation of a successful outcome has been difficult for several reasons, including the diversity of symptoms used for patient selection, unsystematic follow-up, and incomplete descriptions or evaluations of other treatments administered to the patients studied.

There is substantial evidence that *some* pathologic irritability and aggressive acting-out is related to brain pathology. As mentioned earlier, tumors or other irritants of certain brain regions, especially the limbic and associated structures, often facilitate aggressive behavior. And even in the absence of specific lesions, individuals manifesting the "behavioral dyscontrol syndrome" often have disturbed EEG patterns originating in the limbic system. Surgical removal of such regions may result in the alleviation of the pathologic behavior but not without danger to the individual. Psychosurgery is serious, irreversible intervention that often produces intellectual and psychological impairment. Although it is not undertaken lightly, the fact that it is still used indicates the desperation of those who must cope with these serious behavioral problems.

The general concern over violent crimes and frustration with the ineffectiveness of conventional control and treatment has stimulated a growing scientific interest in all forms of aggressive acting-out behavior in other, *nonmedically* defined individuals and has led to pressure for the wider application of psychosurgery in prisons and even in the general population. Some are so convinced that there are brain regions specifically devoted to regulating the expression of violence that they have proposed surgery even in the absence of evidence of pathology to excise the regions of the brain that regulate undesirable behavior [19].

There is also a growing feeling in some circles that "just as there are wild cats and wild monkeys, there are wild men," who have been assumed to "have so much spontaneous activity in the neural systems which underlie aggressive behavior that they are a constant threat to themselves and to those around them" [109]. In the absence of data drawn from experimentation with human subjects, arbitrary or inappropriate generalization from animal data to the human condition has led to the impression that a great amount of human violence is probably triggered by abnormality in the brain and that brain disease may be implicated even in riots and urban violence. Such thinking has resulted in a call for wider testing of limbic system function so as to locate individuals in the general population who are easily triggered to impulsive violence [97].

Critical Organ Surgery

There have been other kinds of surgical intervention such as "critical organ surgery"—i.e., castration—that have been applied primarily to chronic sexual offenders. The rationale for this intervention is based on observations mostly in animals, suggesting an endocrine basis for aggressive behavior. Specifically, the male androgen, testosterone, organizes not only the physical and physiological nature of males, but also those functions of the brain concerned with "male" behavior, including a more aggressive acting-out behavior than is found in females. Sturup has described castration to reduce sex-related aggressiveness in men as "therapeutic castration," as opposed to "judicial castration," a punishment for sex crimes [156]. Therapeutic castration originally was used in the United States to subdue the sexual urge of prisoners [83]. These surgical procedures, legalized in 1907, were abolished as unconstitutional in 1921. Therapeutic castration is still practiced legally in several European countries, mostly on a voluntary basis. Castration in most cases seems to diminish the libido [179], but it has no influence on perversion [154, 155].

Drug Treatments

The effects of therapeutic castration often can be duplicated by reversible chemical means, that is, by hormone treatment. Such treatments today have been applied most often to the aggressive sexual offender. Estrogens have been used to control deviant behavior in men for more than twenty years [41, 50, 110, 175]. Although animal experiments have suggested that estrogens can reduce aggressive acting out, unpleasant and potentially serious side effects have precluded further use of such hormones in humans. For a time, progestins were employed because they inhibited testicular functions without the feminizing effects of estrogens. However, since chronic administration of progesterone may lead to irreversible testicular atrophy, a new compound developed in the late 1960s, cyproterone, which acts effectively yet reversibly, is applied increasingly in the treatment of sexually aggressive offenders [62, 82]. This compound is one of several anti-androgens that effectively control libido, sex drive, and sex behavior and performance, and that reduce or eliminate sexual behavior in the human male. The actions are reversible; harmful side effects, such as general feminization and obesity, appear to be minimal. Under such circumstances a therapeutic approach involving anti-androgens is more likely to be accepted than irreversible interventions such as castration. Ferracuti and Bartilotti confirm this conclusion in their recent review of some of the complex social, methodological, and legal problems involved with the utilization of anti-androgens in the treatment of the sex offender [40].

Knowledge of the chemistry of the brain and its functional dependence on various endogenous substances including hormones, neurotransmitters, foodstuffs, and others has increased rapidly in recent years. Some behavioral abnormalities have been associated with specific chemical defects and many more have been proposed. Whether or not it is correct, this point of view has generated great activity among pharmacologists to develop drugs that modify nervous system mechanisms. A considerable number of these have proved sufficiently potent and safe to permit their use to control human behavior. In recent years, therefore, psychosurgery has been increasingly replaced by drug treatment, the effects of which usually can be adjusted or reversed.

Thus feelings of hostility and tendencies to act out can be reduced by drugs just as they are by lesions. As in the case of lesions, there is not—nor is there likely to be—a specific antihostility agent. Since the causes of hostility in humans vary greatly, the success of drug intervention must likewise vary. But drug intervention is usually reversible, and its side effects are more manageable than surgical procedures.

A number of psychotropic drugs have the ability to ameliorate aggressive tendencies. According to Resnick [135], "psychotropic drugs now available may help indivudals who are aggressive, irritable, unstable, egocentric, easily offended, obsessive, compulsive, and dependent, who demonstrate such symptoms as anxiety, depression, hysteria, agony, unexplainable and motiveless behavior, recurrent violent emotional upset including temper tantrums and violent rages."

The introduction of antipsychotic drugs, such as the phenothiazines, into psychiatry dramatically reduced psychotic hostility in institutions [75]. As a consequence, management of dangerous patients by means of drugs quickly overtook management by surgery or even heavy sedation. Over and above their sedative actions, antipsychotic drugs such as chlorpromazine tame violent humans and reduce other psychotic symptoms. Newer and more potent phenothiazines and butyrophenones have even less sedative side effects [20]. Such agents have also been employed in a variety of conditions in which aggression is displayed in mental defectives, certain types of depressives, sexual deviants, alcoholics, and disturbed adolescent and hyperactive children.

The association of acting out aggressive behavior with possible subcortical EEG abnormalities has led to the use of antiseizure drugs to control hyperexcitability and hostility in children with severe behavior disorders as well as in psychiatric patients displaying, among other symptoms, anger, irritability, and tension. Other treatable symptoms include explosiveness, low frustration tolerance, irritability, impulsive behavior, compulsive behavior, aggressive behavior, erratic behavior, inability to delay gratification, mood swings, short attention spans, and undirected activity [134].

Treatment of hyperkinetic children by drugs that cause mood arousal often reduces symptoms that include aggressiveness, temper tantrums, and impulsiveness. This result is a startling paradox that is not yet well understood. These drugs may sometimes be useful in treating adults with immature personalities who display outbursts of spontaneous aggression [6].

Lithium chloride, an agent used to control episodic mania and depression, has been reported to decrease combative behavior in subjects who did not suffer from affective disorders [108, 150]. Minor tranquilizers that are especially nontoxic and that can tame violent cats and monkeys also control the symptoms of tension and anxiety associated with irritable humans. The more effective of these drugs, the benzodiazepines (chlordiazepoxide and diazepam), effectively reduce aggressive excitability, hostility, and irritability at dose levels that cause minimal sedation and ataxia.

Where management and institutional peacefulness are the main goals of institutions, it is now possible to regulate the behaviors of substantial numbers of people by currently available drugs. And indeed, the astonishingly ubiquitous use of minor tranquilizers suggests that for some the "future is now."

The current surgical and chemical interventions are based on a "sick-brain, sick-behavior" philosophy. And to be sure, some abnormal acting-out behavior probably stems from specific abnormal activity in the human communication systems, both nervous and endocrine. Such interventions, based on careful diagnosis of disease, clearly are useful [27]. Nevertheless, today's psychotropic drugs, employed much like relatively unspecific surgical probes, are exogenous chemical probes used chiefly to manage rather than to treat specific offensive and destructive behaviors. They do have substantial advantages over surgical methods in that their effects are adjustable and reversible, and the side effects are more tolerable. Some have even been used to make subjects more manageable and accessible in behavior modification programs [134]. But the relationship between brain abnormalities and violent behavior in prisoners, for example, is relatively infrequent [96, 165], and it is unlikely that the relationship would be any better in the general population.

Like other behaviors, aggressive behavior is strongly influenced by experience. And also like other behaviors, its expression or inhibition in both animals and human beings can be reinforced. For most men and women who commit violent offenses, the crucial factor is probably the influence of hostile environment rather than some inherent abnormality that makes them different. Therefore surgical or chemical suppression of physiological mechanisms involved in acting-out behavior in these individuals is palliative at best. Despite the promise and relative safety of pharmacologic agents, *selective* treatment of aggressive behavior with drugs has been used in relatively small numbers of patients in relatively uncontrolled experiments. The promise has yet to be fulfilled.

In recent years, the biochemical view of the organization of the brain and, consequently, of behavior has become more sophisticated. Interest has turned to mechanisms by which the body regulates its own behavior states. As noted previously, this has been faciliated by discoveries of normally secreted short-chain polypeptide substances that appear to mediate functions of the brain such as facilitation of aversive learning, memory retrieval, appreciation of pain, altered arousal states, as well as modification of the sensitivity of certain brain sites to the actions of the better known amine neurotransmitters.

In the light of this new information regarding the internal chemical mechanisms employed by the body to translate experiential input into biologic information and to condition its own future behavior, it seems reasonable that new tools may soon be available to facilitate the speed and effectiveness of the modification of behavior. Such substances are relatively easy to synthesize, and the list of stable analogs of these endogenous compounds grows daily. The list of applications of these substances to both animal and human behavior is likewise growing. For example, fragments of the peptide hormone ACTH, which facilitate retrieval and attentional processes in animals [12, 23, 30] are being studied for possible utility in the treatment of memory deficits in the aged [169] and in certain learning disabilities in children [141]. Some peptides seem to be especially effective in inhibiting the extinction of experimentally learned behaviors. Moreover, their toxicities and side effects are extremely low. Such substances, therefore, ought to be especially useful adjuncts in behavior modification programs.

This approach is a qualitatively different alternative to lesions and conventional chemotherapy. It proposes to alter aggressive behavior not by interfering with the physiological bases of acting-out behavior but rather by effectively facilitating its conditioned suppression together with physiologic reinforcement of socially acceptable behavior. The utility of this idea has not escaped the attention of a number of laboratories in both the United States and Europe.

The Coming Model of Biomedical Intervention

Despite the increasing specificity of biomedical knowledge about the origin and control of violence, the intervention techniques for the application of this knowledge reflect little theoretical sophistication. Wolpe [180] is certainly correct in declaring that "as every experienced clinician knows, it is trial and error that ultimately decides which drugs (or any intervention) will be effective in any individual case." Acceptance of these unconventional therapeutic approaches has depended not only on the tortuous process of trial and error but also on serendipity and on the changing public and professional attitudes toward the resources of surgery and pharmacology. A canon of expectations will gradually be assembled. What is certain is that future methods will be radical departures from present methods.

It is fashionable to reject the medical or rehabilitative model as inappropriate and ineffective for the treatment of offenders. The prevailing wisdom in one line of thought holds that *desert* is the only justification for the control and detention of any offender. Another view that is gaining wide acceptance is that of Wilson [177], who believes that dangerous offenders must be restrained to protect society from victimization rather than to punish or rehabilitate.

Perhaps these views are too sweeping, taking too little account of the immense variety of personal conditions that offenders bring with them to the prison. No one can declare that a medical intervention can be found for the treatment of every dangerous offender. Indeed, most of the street crime that terrifies our blighted cities must be attributed to social causes that no physician can hope to address. Nevertheless, there are the foundations of hope in the new and increasingly specific medical perspectives discussed in this chapter. For some chronic offenders who now spend long years in maximum custody conditions, hope is real. Because interventions of this kind are foreseeable and efficient, the oppressive control that justifies the fortress-prison will be infrequently needed.

Hope can return to the prison through understanding of the biological substrates that underlie violent behavior. But there is also a new terror in this prospect. Hitherto, for example, clinicians have had to rely on the processes of aging to bring about the extinction of dangerous behavior. But peptide intervention, along the lines suggested here, may hasten the learning of new behavior patterns so that long years in maximum security control can be cut short, but without diminishing the prisoner's vitality and potential contributions.

But if there is hope for the prisoner's successful reintegration through the administration of neuropeptides, there may also be other potentialities of which the clinician and the policy-maker must take account. In the interests of individual autonomy, liberal political observers have resisted the application of physiological controls, even for the most aggressive prisoner. Their caution is both understandable and justified. For if these new interventions can quench the aggression that is so fearful in our cities, what else can they do? What other controls that may limit freedom and constrain individuality may be applied under the same paradigm to more innocent members of society? No one knows for sure, and no one has seriously considered the ethical and legal curbs that may be necessary to protect us from the abuse.

Nevertheless, a dramatic change in the correctional apparatus is foreseeable. As the uncontrollably violent person learns to tame himself, confidence in the potentialities of active intervention will be regained and the community will not have to rely exclusively on tranquilizers, sedatives, and other such psychoactive agents and on the mechanical constraints of walls, concertina wire, and tempered steel. The clockwork can be adjusted, and as we learn the necessary skills, the specter of horrifying abuse inevitably arises. It is not too early to initiate an examination of the principles that society must enforce if what is done to the prisoner to enable him to live is not to be done to the citizen to assure that he does as his masters tell him. At this perplexing point the scientist and the clinician must invite the moral philosopher to assist in the definition of the new limits of clockwork.

References

1. V.C. Abrahams, S.M. Hilton, and A. Zbrozyna. "Active Muscle Vaso-dilation Produced by Stimulation of the Brainstem: Its Significance in the Defence Reaction." *Journal of Physiology* 154: 491, 1960.

2. R.B. Aird. "Clinical Syndromes of the Limbic System." *International Journal of Neurology* 6: 340, 1968.

3. B.J. Alpers. "Relation of the Hypothalamus to Disorders of Personality: Report of a Case." *Archives of Neurological Psychiatry* 38: 391, 1937.

4. E. Anderson and W. Haymaker. "Breakthroughs in Hypothalamic and Pituitary Research." *Progress in Brain Research* 41: 1, 1974.

5. M. Antonita, C.L. Scudder, and A.G. Karczmar. "The Effect of Norethynodrel with Mestranol Treatment of Female Mice on the Isolation-Induced Aggression of Their Male Offspring." *Pharmacologist* 10: 168, 1968.

6. T.A. Ban. *Psychopharmacology*. Baltimore: Williams and Wilkins, 1969.

7. R.J. Bandler and K.E. Moyer. "Animals Spontaneously Attacked by Rats." *Communications in Behavioral Biology* 5: 177, 1970.

8. P. Bard. "A Diencephalic Mechanism for the Expression of Rage with Special Reference to the Sympathetic Nervous System." *American Journal of Physiology* 84: 490, 1928.

9. P. Bard. "The Ontogenesis of One Physiologist." *Annual Review of Physiology* 35: 1, 1973.

10. P. Bard and V.B. Mountcastle. "Some Forebrain Mechanisms Involved in Expression of Rage with Special Reference to Suppression of Angry Behavior." *Research Publications of the Association for Nervous and Mental Disorders* 27: 362, 1948.

11. B.L. Baxter. "Comparison of Behavioral Effects of Electrical or Chemical Stimulation Applied at the Same Brain Loci." *Experiments in Neurology* 19: 412, 1967.

12. B.E. Beckwith, C.A. Sandman, and A.J. Kastin. "Influence of Three Short-Chain Peptides (α-MSH, MSH/ACTH 4-9, MIF-1) on Dimensional Attention." In *The Neuropeptides*, ed. by C.A. Sandman, L.H. Miller, and A.J. Kastin, *Pharmacology Biochemistry and Behavior* 5: Supp. 1, 11, 1976.

13. E.A. Beeman. "The Effect of Male Hormone on Aggressive Behavior in Mice." *Physiological Zoology* 0: 373, 1947.

14. J.M. Bevan, W. Bevan, and B.F. Williams. "Spontaneous Aggressiveness in Young Castrate C^{3}H Male Mice Treated with Three Dose Levels of Testosterone." *Physiological Zoology* 31: 284, 1958.

15. W. Bevan, G.W. Levy, J.M. Whitehouse, and J.M. Bevan. "Spontaneous Aggressiveness in Two Strains of Mice Castrate and Treated with One of Three Androgens." *Physiological Zoology* 30: 341, 1957.

16. E.L. Bliss, J. Ailion, and J. Zwanziger. "Metabolism of Norepinephrine, Serotonin and Dopamine in Rat Brain with Stress." *Journal of Pharmacology and Experimental Therapeutics* 164: 122, 1968.

17. D. Blumer. "Changes of Sexual Behavior Related to Temporal Lobe Disorders in Man." *Journal of Sex Research* 6: 173, 1970.

18. J. Bremer. *Asexualization: A Follow-Up Study of 244 Cases.* New York: Macmillan, 1959.

19. M.H. Brown. "Further Experience with Multiple Limbic Lesions for Schizophrenia and Sociopathic Aggression." Presented at the Third World Congress of Psychosurgery (Cambridge, England, August 14-19, 1972).

20. R. Byck. "Drugs and the Treatment of Psychiatric Disorders." In *The Pharmacological Basis of Therapeutics*, 5th ed., ed. by L.S. Goodman and A. Gilman. New York: Macmillan, 1975, chap. 12.

21. W.B. Cannon. *Bodily Changes in Pain, Hunger, Fear and Rage*, 2nd ed., College Park, Md.: McGrath, 1970.

22. W.B. Cannon and S.W. Britton. "Studies on the Conditions of Activity in Endocrine Glands. XV. Pseudoaffective Medulliadrenal Secretion." *American Journal of Physiology* 72: 283, 1925.

23. T.F. Champney, T.L. Sakley, and C.A. Sandman. "Effects of Neonatal Cerebral Ventricular Injection of ACTH 4-9 and Subsequent Adult Injections on Learning in Male and Female Albino Rats." In *The Neuropeptides*, ed. by C.A. Sandman, L.H. Miller, and A.J. Kastin, *Pharmacology, Biochemistry and Behavior* 5: supp. 1, 3, 1976.

24. C.D. Clemente and M.H. Chase. "Neurological Substrates of Aggressive Behavior." *Annual Reviews of Physiology* 35: 329, 1973.

25. R.L. Conner and S. Levine. "Hormonal Influences on Aggressive Behavior." In *Aggressive Behavior*, ed. by S. Garattini and E.B. Sigg. Amsterdam: Excerpta Medica Foundation, 1969, p. 150.

26. R.L. Conner, J.M. Stolk, J.D. Barchas, W.C. Dement, and S. Levine. "The Effect of Parachlorophenylalanine (PCPA) on Shock-Induced Fighting Behavior in Rats." *Physiology and Behavior* 5: 1221, 1970.

27. B.J. Culliton. "Psychosurgery: National Commission Issues Surprisingly Favorable Report." *Science* 194: 299, 1976.

28. R.D. Currier, S.C. Little, J.F. Suess, and J.D. Andy. "Sexual Seizures." *Archives of Neurology* 25: 260, 1971.

29. D.E. Davis and L.V. Domm. "The Influence of Hormones on the Sexual Behavior of Domestic Fowl." In *Essays in Biology*, in honor of Herbert M. Evans, written by his friends. Berkeley, Calif.: University of California Press, 1943, p. 171.

30. D. DeWeid. "Pituitary-Adrenal System Hormones and Behaviors." In *The Neurosciences, 3rd Study Program*, ed. by F.O. Schmitt and F.G. Worden. Cambridge, Mass.: MIT Press, 1974.

31. C.W. Dunn. "Stibesterol-Induced Testicular Degeneration in Hypersexual Males." *Journal of Clinical Endocrinology* 1: 643, 1941.

32. J.G. Dusser De Barenne. "Recherches Experimentales sur les Fonctions du Systeme Nerveux Central, Faties en Particulier sur Deux Chat Dont le

Neopallidum Avait Ete Enleve." *Archives Neerlandaises de Physiologie* 4: 31, 1920.

33. G.D. Ellison and J.P. Flynn. "Organized Aggressive Behavior in Cats After Surgical Isolation of the Hypothalamus." *Archives Italiennes de Biologie* 106: 1, 1968.

34. A.W. Epstein. "Disordered Human Sexual Behavior Associated with Temporal Lobe Dysfunction." *Medical Aspects of Human Sexuality* 3: 62, 1969.

35. L.T. Evans. "Social Behavior of the Normal and Castrated Lizard, *Anolis Carolinensis.*" *Science* 83: 104, 1936.

36. G.M. Everett and R.G. Wiegand. "Non-hydrazide Monoamine Oxidase Inhibitors and Their Effects on Central Amines and Motor Behavior." *Biochemical Pharmacology* 8: 163, 1961.

37. G.M. Everett and J.W. Borcherding. "L-Dopa: Effect on Concentrations of Dopamine, Norepinephrine and Serotonin in Brains of Mice." *Science* 168: 849, 1970.

38. J. Ferguson, S. Henrikson, J. Cohen, G. Mitchel, J. Barchas, and W. Dement. "Hypersexuality and Behavioral Changes in Cats Caused by Administration of *p*-Chlorophenylanine." *Science* 168: 499, 1970.

39. A. Fernandez De Molina and R.W. Hunsperger. "Organization of the Subcortical System Governing Defense and Flight Reactions in the Cat." *Journal of Physiology (Lond.)* 160: 200, 1962.

40. F. Ferracuti and R. Bartilotti. "Technical and Legal Aspects in the Pharmacologic Treatment of Sex Offenders." In *Sexual Behavior: Pharmacology and Biochemistry*, ed. by M. Sandler and G.L. Gessa. New York: Raven Press, 1975, p. 205.

41. L.H. Field and M. Williams. "The Hormonal Treatment of Sexual Offenders." *Medicine, Science and the Law* 10: 27, 1970.

42. J.P. Flynn, H. Vanegas, W. Foote, and S. Edwards. "Neural Mechanisms Involved in a Cat's Attack on a Rat." In *Neural Control of Behavior*, ed. by R.E. Whalen, R.F. Thompson, M. Verzeans, and N.F. Weinberger. New York: Academic Press, 1970, p. 135.

43. E. Fredericson, A.W. Story, N.L. Gurney, and K. Butterworth. "The Relationship Between Heredity, Sex, and Aggression in Two Inbred Mouse Strains." *Journal of Genetic Psychology* 87: 121, 1955.

44. J.F. Fulton. "Contemporary Concepts of the Hypothalamus and Their Origin." *Quarterly Bulletin of the Northwestern University Medical School* 28: 10, 1954.

45. B.E. Ginsburg and W.C. Allec. "Some Effects Conditioning on Social Dominance and Subordination in Inbred Strains of Mice." *Physiological Zoology* 15: 485, 1942.

46. M. Glusman. "The Hypothalamic 'Savage' Syndrome." In *Aggression*,

ed. by S.H. Frazier. *Research Publications of the Association for Nervous and Mental Diseases* 52: 52, 1974. Baltimore, Md.: Williams and Wilkins.

47. H.H. Goddard. *The Kallikak Family, A Study of the Heredity of Feeblemindedness.* New York: Macmillan, 1913.

48. A. Goldstein. "Opiod Peptides (Endorphins) in Pituitary and Brain." *Science* 193: 1081, 1976.

49. M. Goldstein. "Brain Research and Violent Behavior." *Archives of Neurology* 30: 1, 1974.

50. F.L. Golla and R.S. Hodge. "Hormone Treatment of the Sexual Offender." *Lancet* 1: 1006, 1949.

51. F. Goltz. "Der Hund ohne Grosshirn." *Pfluger's Archive fur die gesamte Physiologie des Menschen und der Tiere* 51: 570, 1892.

52. L.M. Gunne and T. Lewander. "Monoamines in Brain and Adrenal Glands of Cat After Electrically Induced Defense Reaction." *Acta Physiologica Scandinavica* 67: 405, 1966.

53. R.G. Heath, R.R. Monroe, and W.A. Mickle. "Stimulation of the Amygdaloid Nucleus in a Schizophrenic Patient." *American Journal of Psychiatry* 111: 862, 1955.

54. R. Hernandez-Peon, G. Chavez-Ibarra, P.J. Morgane, and C. Timo-Iaria. "Limbic Cholinergic Pathways Involved in Sleep and Emotional Behavior." *Experimental Neurology* 8: 93, 1963.

55. W.R. Hess. *Das Zwishenhirn: Syndrome, Lokalisationen, Funktionen.* Basel: Schwabe, 1949.

56. W.R. Hess. *Diencephalon: Autonomic and Extrapyramidal Functions.* New York: Grune and Stratton, 1954.

57. W.R. Hess. *The Functional Organization of the Diencephalon.* New York: Grune and Stratton, 1957.

58. W.R. Hess and M. Brügger. "Das subkortikale Zentrum der affektiven Abwehrreaktion." *Helvetica Physiologica et Pharmacologica acta* 1: 33, 1943.

59. W.R. Hess and K. Akert. "Experimental Data on Role of Hypothalamus in Mechanisms of Emotional Behavior." *AMA Archives of Neurology and Psychiatry* 73: 127, 1955.

60. D. Hill. "Cerebral Dysrhythmia: Its Significance in Aggressive Behavior." *Proceedings of the Royal Society of Medicine* 37: 317, 1944.

61. D. Hill and D. Watterson. "Electro-encephalographic Studies of Psychopathic Personalities." *Journal of Neurology and Psychiatry* 5: 47, 1942.

62. H. Hoffet. "On the Application of the Testosterone Blocker Cyproterone Acetate (SH 714) in Sex Deviants and Psychiatric Patients in Institutions." *Praxis* 7: 221, 1968.

63. L. Hofstatter and M. Girgis. "Depth Electrode Investigations of the

Limbic System of the Brain by Radiostimulation, Electrolytic Lesion and Histochemical Studies." Presented at the *Third International Congress of Psychosurgery*, Cambridge, England, 1972.

64. Z.P. Horovitz, P.W. Ragazzino, and R.C. Leaf. "Selective Block of Rat Mouse-Killing by Antidepressants." *Life Sciences* 4: 1909, 1965.

65. R.W. Hunsperger. "Affektreakionen auf electrische Reizung in Hernstamm der Katze." *Helvetica Physiologica et Pharmacologica acta* 14: 70, 1956.

66. R.R. Hutchinson, R. Ulrich, and N.H. Azrin. "Effects of Age and Related Factors on the Rain-Aggression Reaction." *Journal of Comparative and Physiological Psychology* 59: 365, 1965.

67. C.F. Jacobsen. "Studies of Cerebral Function in Primates." *Comparative Psychology Monograph* 13: 1, 1936.

68. B. Kaada. "Brain Mechanisms Related to Aggressive Behavior." In *Brain Function, vol. 5. Aggression and Defense: Neural Mechanisms and Social Patterns*, ed. by C.D. Clemente and D.B. Lindsley. Los Angeles: University of California Press, 1967, p. 95.

69. H. Kabat, B.J. Anson, H.W. Magoun, and S.W. Ranson. "Stimulation of the Hypothalamus with Special Reference to Its Effects on Gastro-Intestinal Motility." *American Journal of Physiology* 112: 214, 1935.

70. A.J. Kastin, N.P. Plotinikoff, A.V. Schally, and C.A. Sandman. "Endocrine and CNS Effects of Hypothalamic Peptides and MSH." In *Reviews of Neuroscience*, vol. 2, ed. by S. Ehrenpreis and I.J. Kopin. New York: Raven Press, 1976, p. 111.

71. A.J. Kastin, R.H. Ehrensing, D.S. Schalch, and M.S. Anderson. "Improvement in Mental Depression with Decreased Thyrotropin Response After Administration of Thyrotropin-Releasing Hormone." *Lancet* 2: 740, 1972.

72. F. Kennedy. "The Hypothalamus." *Journal of the American Medical Association* 114: 2092, 1940.

73. S.S. Kety, F. Javoy, A-M. Thierry, I. Julow, and A. Glowinski. "A Sustained Effect of Electroconvulsive Shock on the Turnover of Norepinephrine in the Central Nervous System of Rats." *Proceedings of the National Academy of Science* 58: 1249, 1967.

74. M.B. King and B.G. Haebel, "Killing Elicited by Brain Stimulation in Rats." *Communications in Behavioral Biology* 2: 173, 1968.

75. N.S. Kline. "Drugs Are the Greatest Practical Advance in the History of Psychiatry." *New Medica Materia. For Diagnosis, Prevention, Treatment* 4: 48, 1962.

76. H. Kluver and P.C. Burg. "Preliminary Analysis of the Functions of the Temporal Lobes in Monkeys." *Archives of Neurology and Psychiatry* 42: 979, 1939.

77. L.E. Kreuz and R.M. Rose. "Assessment of Aggressive Behavior and

Plasma Testosterone in a Young Criminal Population." *Psychosomatic Medicine* 34: 321, 1972.

78. A.S. Kulkarni. "Muricidal Block Produced by 5-Hydroxytryptophan and Various Drugs." *Life Sciences* 7: 125, 1968.

79. H. Lal, B. Nesson, and N. Smith. "Amphetamine-Induced Aggression in Mice Pretreated with Dihydroxyphenylalmine (DOPA) and/or Reserpine." *Biological Psychiatry* 2: 299, 1970.

80. H. Lal, J.J. DeFeo, and P. Thut. "Effect of Amphetamine on Pain-Induced Aggression." *Communications in Behavioral Biology* 1: 333, 1968.

81. F. Lamprecht, B.S. Eichelman, N.B. Thoa, R.B. Williams, and I.J. Kopin. "Rat Fighting Behavior Serum Dopamine-β-Hydroxylase and Hypothalamic Tyrosine Hydroxylase." *Science* 177: 1214, 1972.

82. U. Laschet. "Antiandrogens in the Treatment of Sex Offenders: Mode of Action and Therapeutic Outcome." In *Contemporary Sexual Behavior: Critical Issues in the 1970's*, ed. by J. Zubin and J. Money. Baltimore, Md.: Johns Hopkins University Press, 1973.

83. L. LeMaire. "Danish Experiences Regarding the Castration of Sexual Offenders." *Journal of Criminal Law* 46: 294, 1956.

84. J.V. Levy. "The Effects of Testosterone Propionate on Fighting Behavior in $C_{57}B1$-10 Young Female Mice." *Proceedings of the West Virginia Academy of Science* 26: 14, 1954.

85. T. Lewander. "Urinary Excretion and Tissue Levels of Catecholamines During Chronic Amphetamine Intoxication." *Psychopharmacologia* 13: 394, 1968.

86. C.W. Lloyd. "Problems Associated with the Menstrual Cycle." In *Human Reproduction and Sexual Behavior*, ed. by C.W. Lloyd. Philadelphia: Lea and Febiger, 1964, p. 288.

87. E. Lycke, K. Modigh, and B.F. Roos. "Aggression in Mice Associated with Changes in the Monoamine-Metabolism of the Brain." *Experientia* 25: 951, 1969.

88. P.D. MacLean. "Psychosomatic Disease and the 'visceral brain,' Recent Developments Bearing on the Papez Theory of Emotion." *Psychosomatic Medicine* 11: 338, 1949.

89. P.D. MacLean. "Some Psychiatric Implications of Physiological Studies of Frontotemporal Portion of Limbic System (Visceral Brain)." *Electroencephalography and Clinical Neurophysiology* 4: 407, 1952.

90. P.D. MacLean. "Chemical and Electrical Stimulation of Hippocampus in Unrestrained Animals. II. Behavioral Findings." *AMA Archives of Neurology and Psychiatry* 78: 128, 1957.

91. P.D. MacLean. "The Limbic System with Respect to Self-Preservation and the Preservation of the Species." *Journal of Nervous Mental Disease* 127: 1, 1958.

92. P.D. MacLean. "The Hypothalamus and Emotional Behavior." In *The Hypothalamus*, ed. by W. Haymaker, E. Anderson, and W.J.H. Nauta. Springfield, Ill.: Charles C. Thomas, 1969, chapter 8.

93. P.D. MacLean. "Implications of Microelectrode Findings on Exteroceptive Inputs into the Limbic Cortex." In *Limbic System Mechanisms and Autonomic Function*, ed. by C.H. Hockman. Springfield, Ill.: Charles C. Thomas, 1972.

94. H.W. Magoun. *The Waking Brain*. Springfield, Ill.: Charles C. Thomas, 1958.

95. H.W. Magoun, R.W. Barris, and S.W. Ranson. "Stimulation of the Hypothalamus with the Horsley-Clarke Instrument." *Anatomical Record* (supp. 24), 1932.

96. V.H. Mark, W.H. Sweet, and F.R. Ervin. "Role of Brain Disease in Riots and Urban Violence." *Journal of the American Medical Association* 201: 895, 1967.

97. V.H. Mark and F.R. Ervin. *Violence and the Brain*. New York: Harper & Row, 1970.

98. J.L. Marx. "Learning and Behavior (I): Effects of Pituitary Hormones." *Science* 190: 367, 1975.

99. J.L. Marx. "Learning and Behavior (II): The Hypothalamic Peptides." *Science* 190: 544, 1975.

100. J.H. Masserman. "Is the Hypothalamus a Center of Emotion?" *Psychosomatic Medicine* 3: 3, 1941.

101. J.H. Masserman. *Behavior and Neurosis. An Experimental Psychoanalytic Approach to Psychobiologic Principles*. Chicago: University of Chicago Press, 1943.

102. R.P. Michael. "Effects of Gonadal Hormones on Displaced and Direct Aggression in Pairs of Rhesus Monkeys of Opposite Sex." In *Aggressive Behavior*, ed. by S. Garattini and E.B. Sigg. Amsterdam: Excerpta Medica Foundation, 1969, p. 172.

103. L.H. Miller, L.C. Harris, H. VanRiezen, and A.J. Kastin. "Neuroheptapeptide Influence on Attention and Memory in Man." In *The Neuropeptides*, ed. by C.A. Sandman, L.H. Miller, and A.J. Kastin. *Pharmacology, Biochemistry and Behavior* 5: supp. 1, 17, 1976.

104. A.F. Mirsky. "The Influence of Sex Hormones on Social Behavior in Monkeys." *Journal of Comparative and Physiological Psychology* 48: 327, 1955.

105. J. Money. "Use of an Androgen-Depleting Hormone in the Treatment of Male Sex Offenders." *Journal of Sex Research* 6: 165, 1970.

106. E. Moniz. "How I Succeeded in Performing the Prefrontal Leukotomy." In *The Great Psychodynamic Therapies in Psychiatry*, ed. by A. Sackler, M. Sackler, R. Sackler, and F. Marti-Ibanez. New York: Harper & Row, 1956, p. 131.

107. R.H. Moos, B.S. Kopell, F.T. Melges, I.D. Yalom, D.T. Lunde, R.B. Clayton, and D.A. Hamburg. "Fluctuations in Symptoms and Moods During the Menstrual Cycle." *Journal of Psychosomatic Research (London)* 13: 37, 1969.

108. S.D. Morrison, C.W. Erwin, D.T. Gianturco, and C.J. Gerber. "Effect of Lithium on Combative Behavior in Humans." *Diseases of the Nervous System* 34: 186, 1973.

109. K.E. Moyer. "The Physiology of Aggression and the Implications of Aggression Control." In *The Control of Aggression and Violence: Cognitive and Physiological Factors*, ed. by J.L. Singer. New York: Academic Press, 1971, p. 61.

110. M.A.F. Murray, J.H.J. Bancroft, D.C. Anderson, T.G. Tennent, and P.J. Carr. "Endocrine Changes in Male Sexual Deviants After Treatment with Anti-Androgens, Oestrogens or Tranquilizers." *Journal of Endocrinology* 67: 179, 1975.

111. R.D. Myers. "Emotional and Autonomic Responses Following Hypothalamic Chemical Stimulation." *Canadian Journal of Psychology* 18: 6, 1964.

112. H. Narabayashi. "Stereotaxic Amygdalectomy." In *The Neurobiology of the Amygdala*, ed. by B.E. Eleftheriou. New York: Plenum Press, 1972, p. 459.

113. W.J.H. Nauta. "The Central Viseromotor System: A General Survey." In *Limbic System Mechanisms and Autonomic Function*, ed. by C.H. Hackman. Springfield, Ill.: Charles C. Thomas, 1972, p. 21.

114. W.J.H. Nauta and W. Haymaker. "Hypothalamic Nuclei and Fiber Connections." In *The Hypothalamus*, ed. by W. Haymaker, E. Anderson, and W.J.H. Nauta. Springfield, Ill.: Charles C. Thomas, 1969, p. 136.

115. J. Olds. "The Central Nervous System and the Reinforcement of Behavior." *American Psychologist* 34: 114, 1969.

116. J. Panksepp. "Effect of Hypothalamic Lesions on Mouse-Killing and Shock-Induced Fighting in Rats." *Physiology and Behavior* 6: 311, 1971.

117. J. Panksepp. "Aggression Elicited by Electrical Stimulation of the Hypothalamus in Albino Rats." *Physiology and Behavior* 6: 321, 1971.

118. J.W. Papez. "The Human Brain." *Eugenics* 3-4: various pages, 1930-1931.

119. J.W. Papez. "A Proposed Mechanism of Emotion." *Archives of Neurology and Psychiatry* 38: 725, 1937.

120. J.W. Papez. "Cerebral Mechanism." *Journal of Nervous and Mental Disease* 89: 145, 1939.

121. H. Persky, D.K. Smith, and G.K. Basu. "Relation of Psychologic Measures of Aggression and Hostility to Testosterone Production in Man." *Psychosomatic Medicine* 33: 265, 1971.

122. A.J. Prange, I.C. Wilson, P.P. Lara, L.B. Alltop, and G.R. Breese. "Effects of Thyrotropin-Releasing Hormone in Depression." *Lancet* 2: 999, 1972.

123. A. Randrup and I. Munkvad. "DOPA and Other Naturally Occurring Substances as Causes of Stereotypy and Rage in Rats." *Acta Psychiatrica Scandinavica* 42: supp. 191, 193, 1966.

124. A. Randrup and I. Munkvad. "Stereotyped Activities Produced by Amphetamine in Several Animal Species and Man." *Psychopharmacologia* 11: 300, 1967.

125. S.W. Ranson. "The Hypothalamus: Its Significance for Visceral Innervation and Emotional Expression." *Transactions and Studies of the College of Physicians of Philadelphia* 2: 222, 1934.

126. S.W. Ranson. "Some Functions of the Hypothalamus." *Harvey Lectures* 32: 92, 1937.

127. D.J. Reis. "The Relationship Between Brain Norepinephrine and Aggressive Behavior." *Res. Bull. A.R.N.M.D.* 50: 266, 1972.

128. D.J. Reis. "Central Neurotransmitters in Aggression." In *Aggression*, ed. by S.H. Frazier. *Res. Bull. A.R.N.M.D.* 52: 119, 1974. Baltimore: Williams and Wilkins.

129. D.J. Reis and L.M. Gunne. "Brain Catecholamines: Relation to the Defense Reaction Evoked by Amygdaloid Stimulation in the Cat." *Science* 149: 450, 1965.

130. D.J. Reis, M. Miura, M. Weinbren, and L.M. Gunne. "Brain Catecholamines: Relation to Defense Reaction Evoked by Acute Brainstem Transection in Cats." *Science* 156: 1768, 1967.

131. D.J. Reis and K. Fuxe. "Brain Norepinephrine: Evidence That Neuronal Release Is Essential for Sham Rage Behavior Following Brainstem Transection in Cats." *Proceedings of the National Academy of Science* 64: 108, 1969.

132. D.J. Reis, D.T. Moorhead, and N. Merlino. "DOPA-Induced Excitement in Cats and Its Relationship to Brain Norepinephrine Concentrations." *Archives of Neurology* 22: 31, 1970.

133. D.J. Reis, D.T. Moorhead II, M. Rifkin, T. Joh, and M. Goldstein. "Changes in Enzymes Synthesizing Catecholamines Resulting from Hypothalamic Stimulation Producing Attack Behavior in Cats." *Transactions of the American Neurological Association* 95: 104, 1970.

134. O. Resnick. "The Psychoactive Properties of Diphenylhydantoin: Experiences with Prisoners and Juvenile Delinquents." *International Journal of Neuropsychology* 3: supp. 2, S20, 1967.

135. O. Resnick. "Use of Psychotropic Drugs with Criminals." *Psychopharmacology Bulletin* 5: 17, 1969.

136. W.W. Roberts and H.O. Kiess. "Motivational Properties of Hypothalamic Aggression in Cats." *Journal of Comparative and Physiological Psychology* 58: 187, 1964.

137. W.W. Roberts, M.L. Steinberg, and L.W. Means. "Hypothalamic Mechanisms for Sexual, Aggressive and Other Motivational Behaviors in the Opossum, *Didelphis virginiana.*" *Journal of Comparative and Physiological Psychology* 64: 1, 1967.

138. R.M. Rose, I.S. Bernstein, and J.W. Holaday. "Plasma Testosterone, Dominance, Rank, and Aggressive Behavior in a Group of Male Rhesus Monkeys." *Nature* 321: 366, 1971.

139. H. Rothmann. "Zusammenfassender Bericht uber den Rothmannschen grosshirnlasen Hund mach klinischer und anatomischer Untersuchung." *Zentralblatte fur die Gesamte Neurologie und Psychiatrie* 87: 247, 1923.

140. A. Salama and M.E. Goldberg. "Neurochemical Effects of Imiprimine and Amphetamine in Aggressive Mouse-Killing (Muricidal Rats)." *Biochemical Pharmacology* 19: 2023, 1970.

141. C.A. Sandman, J. George, B.B. Walker, J.D. Nolan, and A.J. Kastin. "Neuropeptide MSH/ACTH 4-10 Enhances Attention in the Mentally Retarded." In *The Neuropeptides*, ed. by C.A. Sandman, L.H. Miller, and A.J. Kastin. *Pharmacology, Biochemistry and Behavior* 5: supp. 1, 23, 1976.

142. Z.A. Sayed, S.A. Lewis, and R.P. Britain. "An Electroencephalographic and Psychiatric Study of 32 Insance Murderers." *Electroencephalography and Clinical Neurophysiology* 27: 335, 1969.

143. J. Scheel-Kruger and A. Randrup. "Stereotyped Hyperactive Behavior Produced by Dopamine in the Absence of Noreadrenaline." *Life Sciences* 6: 1389, 1967.

144. J. Schrold. "Aggressive Behavior in Chicks Induced by Tricyclic Antidepressants." *Psychopharmacologia* 17: 225, 1970.

145. J.P. Scott. "Biological Basis of Human Warfare." In *Interdisciplinary Relationships in the Social Sciences*, ed. by M. Sheriff and C.W. Sheriff. Chicago: Aldine, 1969, p. 121.

146. S.A. Shah and L.H. Roth. "Biological and Pyschological Factors in Criminality." In *Handbook of Criminology*, ed. by D. Glaser. New York: Rand McNally, 1975, pp. 101-173.

147. M.H. Sheard. "The Effect of p-Chlorophenylalanine on Behavior in Rats: Relation to 5-Hydroxytryptamine and 5-Hydroxyindoleacetic Acid." *Brain Research* 15: 524, 1969.

148. M.H. Sheard. "Effect of Lithium on Foot Shock Aggression in Rats." *Nature* 228: 284, 1970.

149. M.H. Sheard. "Behavioral Effects of p-Chlorophenylalanine in Rats: Inhibition by Lithium." *Communications in Behavioral Biology* 5: 71, 1970.

150. M.H. Sheard. "Effect of Lithium on Human Aggression." *Nature* 230: 113, 1971.

151. D.E. Smith, M.B. King, and B.G. Hoebel. "Lateral Hypothalamic Control of Killing: Evidence for a Cholinoceptive Mechanism." *Science* 167: 900, 1970.

152. E.A. Spiegel, H.R. Miller, and M.J. Oppenheimer. "Forebrain and Rage Reactions." *Journal of Neurophysiology* 3: 538, 1940.

153. D. Stafford-Clark and F.H. Taylor. "Clinical and Electro-Encephalographic Studies on Prisoners Charged with Murder." *Journal of Neurology, Neurosurgery and Psychiatry* 12: 325, 1949.

154. G.K. Sturup. "Sexual Offenders and Their Treatment in Denmark and the Other Scandinavian Countries." *International Review of Criminal Policy* 4: 106, 1953.

155. G.K. Sturup. *The Mentally Abnormal Offender.* London: Churchill, 1968, p. 5.

156. G.K. Sturup. "Castration: The Total Treatment." In *Sexual Behaviors: Social, Clinical and Legal Aspects*, ed. by H.L.P. Resnik and M.E. Wolfgang. Boston: Little, Brown, 1972, chap. 18.

157. G.K. Suchowsky, L. Pegrassi, and A. Bonsignori. "The Effect of Steroids on Aggressive Behavior in Isolated Male Mice." In *Aggressive Behavior*, ed. by S. Garattini and E.B. Sigg. Amsterdam: Excerpta Medica Foundation, 1969, p. 164.

158. W.H. Sweet, F.R. Ervin, and V.H. Mark. "The Relationship Between Violent Behavior and Focal Cerebral Disease." In *Aggressive Behavior*, ed. by S. Garattini and E.B. Sigg. Amsterdam: Excerpta Medical Foundation, 1969.

159. A. Tagliomente, P. Tagliomente, G.L. Gessa, and B.B. Brodi. "Compulsive Sexual Activity Induced by p-Chlorophenylalanine in Normal and Pinealectomized Male Rats." *Science* 166: 1433, 1969.

160. A.M. Terdiman and J.V. Levy. "The Effects of Estrogen on Fighting Behavior in Young Male C_{57} F_1-10 Mice." *Proceedings of the West Virginia Academy of Science* 26: 15, 1954.

161. J. Tollman and J.A. King. "The Effects of Testosterone Propionate on Aggression in Male and Female C_{57} BL/10 Mice." *British Journal of Animal Behavior* 4: 147, 1956.

162. B.H. Turner. "Sensorimotor Syndrome Produced by Lesions of the Amygdala and Lateral Hypothalamus." *Journal of Comparative and Physiological Psychology* 82: 34, 1973.

163. E. Ulrich. "The Social Hierarchy in Albino Mice." *Journal of Comparative Psychology* 25: 373, 1938.

164. R. Ulrich. "Pain as a Cause of Aggression." *American Zoologist* 6: 643, 1966.

165. E.S. Valenstein. *Brain Control.* New York: Wiley, 1973, p. 262.

166. L. Valzelli. "Drugs and Aggressiveness." *Advances in Pharmacology* 5: 79, 1967.

167. M.J.E. Van der Vis-Melsen and J.D. Wiener. "Improvement in Mental Depression with Decreased Thyrotropin Response After Administration of Thyrotropin-Releasing Hormone." *Lancet* 2: 1415, 1972.

168. C. VanderWende and M.T. Spoerlein. "Psychotic Symptoms Induced in Mice by the Intravenous Administration of Solutions 3,4-Dihydroxyphenyla-mine (DOPA)." *Archives Internationales de Pharmacodynamie et de Therapie* 137: 145, 1962.

169. Henk van Riezen, personal communication, Bicentennial Neuropeptide Symposium, Philadelphia, April, 1976.

170. C.F. von Economo. *Encephalitis Lethargica: Its Sequele and Treatment,* London: Oxford University Press, 1931.

171. M. Wasman and J.P. Flynn. "Direct Attack Elicited from Hypothalamus." *Archives of Neurology* 6: 220, 1962.

172. M.L. Weischer. "Uber die antiaggressive wirkung von lithium." *Psychopharmacologia* 15: 245, 1969.

173. B.L. Welch and A.S. Welch. "Effects of Grouping on the Level of Brain Norepinephrine in White Swiss Mice." *Life Sciences* 4: 1011, 1965.

174. B.L. Welch and A.S. Welch. "Aggression and the Biogenic Amine Neurohumors." In *Aggressive Behavior*, ed. by S. Garattini and E.B. Sigg. Amsterdam: Excerpta Medica Foundation, 1969, p. 179.

175. L.H. Whittaker. "Oestrogen and Psychosexual Disorders." *Medical Journal of Australia* 2: 547, 1959.

176. D. Williams. "Neural Factors Related to Habitual Aggression." *Brain* 92: 403, 1969.

177. J.Q. Wilson. *Thinking About Crime.* New York: Basic Books, 1975.

178. H.A. Witkin, S.A. Mednick, F. Schulsinger, E. Bakkestrom, K.O. Christiansen, D.R. Goodenough, K. Hirschhorn, C. Lundsteen, D.R. Owen, J. Philip, D.B. Rubin, and M. Stocking. "Criminality in XYY and XXY Men." *Science* 193: 547, 1976.

179. C. Wolfe. *The Castration.* Basel: Benno Schwabe, 1934, p. 16.

180. J. Wolpe. *Psychotherapy by Reciprocal Inhibition.* Palo Alto: Stanford University Press, 1958.

181. C.H. Woodworth. "Attack Elicited in Rats by Electrical Stimulation of the Lateral Hypothalamus." *Physiology and Behavior* 6: 345, 1971.

182. R.S. Woodworth and C.S. Sherrington. "A Pseudoaffective Reflex and Its Spinal Path." *Journal of Physiology* 31: 234, 1904.

The Psychiatric Assessment of Dangerousness: Practical Problems and Political Implications

Stephen Pfohl

In September 1974, a federal district court in Toledo issued an interim order in major "right-to-treatment" litigation on behalf of the 700 patients at Ohio's maximum security hospital for the "criminally insane."[1] A major section of this interim order required the state to seek the diagnostic services of independent mental health professionals to re-evaluate the status of each patient at Lima State Hospital.[2] These specially contracted psychiatric decision-makers were grouped into twelve multidisciplinary review teams. Each team consisted of a psychiatrist, a clinical psychologist, and a psychiatric social worker. Teams were required to decide whether a patient was mentally ill or a psychopathic offender dangerous to self and others and in need of placement in a maximum security facility. Patients would continue to be confined in Lima State Hospital only if they were "immediately dangerous" and needed maximum security or if they were "psychopathic offenders" requiring further treatment.[3]

The work of the patient review teams was important for two reasons. First, their decisions significantly affected the lives and life chances of patient-inmates for years to come. Second, these decisions represented an example of a process widely advocated as a determinant for the use of imprisonment: the assessment and prediction of dangerousness. Indeed, the criterion of dangerousness "has been accepted by two national commissions, by the American Law Institute, by the American Bar Association, by the National Council on Crime and Delinquency in its Model Sentencing Act and its policy statements, by many commentators and in many criminal codes."[4]

Those who favor the psychiatric predictions of dangerousness as justification for confinement in a maximum security facility often refer to the process as if its reliability were objectively verified. Those who carry it out are viewed as expert technicians. These special teams of clinical diagnosticians were accepted as such by criminal justice and mental health officials and by advocates for patients' rights as well. Participants in the litigation leading to the patient reviews were optimistic about the success of psychiatric prediction. Legal advocates representing the patient-plaintiffs were confident that the clinicians recruited for these reviews were the state's "leading experts." According to a

This project was developed in conjunction with a larger study of the methods of psychiatric diagnosticians. It is sponsored, in part, by a grant from the Ohio Division of Mental Health. The author acknowledges the critical and constructive readership of Simon Dinitz, Ron Kramer, Gisela Hinkle, Clyde Franklin, and Diane Vaughan.

Justice Department attorney participating in the case, "The most distinctive part of the order was [that] the Court required people at Lima to be evaluated against some sort of valid standard for commitment to see if all patients really belonged there."[5]

Despite the optimism of those who favor its use, psychiatric prediction finds little empirical support. Research on the prediction of violent behavior does not instill confidence in its reliability. Existing literature consistently reveals very low rates of prognostic accuracy. Whether one develops "predictor scales" based on as many as 100 variables,[6] employs the results of psychological testing, or relies on the judgments of experienced diagnosticians, prediction rates rise no higher than two wrong judgments for every one right judgment.[9] A recent review article on this subject has gone so far as to refer to the prediction process as "flipping coins in the courtroom."[10]

Clearly the predictive process is unreliable. What is at least as serious is its consistent tendency to overpredict failure. "They tend to predict antisocial conduct in many instances where it would not, in fact, occur. Indeed . . . research suggests that for every correct psychiatric prediction of violence, there are numerous erroneous predictions. That is, among every group . . . presently confined on the basis of psychiatric predictions of violence, there are only a few who would, and many more who would not, actually engage in such conduct if released."[11] It is the documentation of such overprediction that led Norval Morris to conclude: "The concept of dangerousness for sentencing purposes is an equivocal principle that leads to gross injustice."[12]

In the wake of considerable doubt about the validity of psychiatric predictions, one cannot view lightly the work of the specially contracted Lima patient review teams. They were asked to do what research suggested they could not have the expertise to do. By considering an individual's past record and assessing present performance, they were to determine whether a patient needed confinement in a maximum security institution. Of what did their considerations and assessments consist? To what degree were decisions reflective of certain "political interests" and diagnosticians' class- or culture-based assumptions? These are the questions with which we are concerned here. If the validity of the prediction of dangerousness is in question, clearly its political significance is not. After all, the essence of such decisions is that the power of the state will be invoked to restrict the future options of those who are considered harmful to the interests of others.

Methodology

Our assessment of the political interests displayed in making decisions about dangerousness and the need for maximum security is derived from a field study of the diagnostic process. To study this process, a group of seven researchers observed the work of the twelve teams of psychiatric professionals in 130 diagnostic sessions. After obtaining informed consents, observers situated themselves as unobtrusively as possible in order to note relevant features of social interaction before, during, and after the evaluation team's interviews of patients. In addition to observers' descriptions of this process, tape recordings and transcripts were made of these selected evaluation sessions.

Furthermore, each participating psychiatric professional was subsequently interviewed regarding his or her impressions, opinions, and reflections of both the patient reviews and the presence of the researcher-observers. An analysis of these materials provides the basis for our interpretation of the political interests involved in predicting dangerousness and the need for maximum security confinement.

Social Characteristics of Psychiatric Professionals Studied

Thirty-seven clinicians participated in the patient review process. Eleven were psychiatrists, thirteen were psychologists, and thirteen were social workers. All were "outside" professionals who were neither employees of Lima State Hospital nor of any other state agency. Some were in private practice. Others worked in community mental health or forensic clinics. Several were affiliated with universities. Nearly all psychiatrists had been recruited directly by the Ohio Commissioner for Forensic Psychiatry, while nearly all the social workers had been recruited by colleagues or by legal advocates for the patient-plaintiffs. Psychologists, who were recruited by either the Forensic Commission or by colleagues, shared with the psychiatrists "considerable past experiences" with patients similar to those they diagnosed at Lima. Most social workers, however, had no past experience with such "maximum security" individuals. In terms of professional orientation, half the clinicians described themselves as "eclectics," and nearly one third stated that they were "psychoanalytically" oriented. Eight of thirty-seven clinicians were women, of whom seven were social workers. All psychiatrists were male. Five of the diagnosticians were blacks. Of these, two were psychiatrists and three were social workers.

How the Predictive Review Teams Viewed Their Own Work

The diagnostic review teams saw their work in a "professional" rather than a political context. Their assessments were viewed in terms of an applied clinical science. They did not regard themselves as judicial arbiters of freedom. Their definition of their work is revealed in the following set of observations.

"Discovery" Versus the Court's Work of "Decision-Making"

The findings of the patient review teams were presented to the federal court, which in principle made the final decision about which patients were to be released, transferred, or retained. In practice, the court, with few exceptions, followed the recommendations of the psychiatric professionals. Nonetheless, the review team members constantly reminded themselves that it was the court that was really deciding on a patient's fate. They were only "discovering" what a patient was really like. This separation between a team's discoveries and a judge's decision is illustrated in the following excerpt.

Excerpt 1. From a Transcript of a Patient Review. (The team is discussing its work in relation to the court's expectations.)

Psychologist: Are we supposed to go for that label or not? Say whether or not they are now psychopathic offenders?
Psychiatrist: I guess so. . . .
Psychologist: If they're a psychopathic offender they're going to stay here?
Psychiatrist: Yes. . . .
Social worker: He said they're all going back to court anyway.
Psychologist: All of these people, whether we label them psychopathic offender or not, are going back to the court anyway?
Psychiatrist: Yes.
Social worker: The're all going back?
Psychologist: What's the difference. . . . Here's a man labeled psychopathic offender and he goes back to court. And a man we say is not a psychopathic offender, and he goes back to court too? Then what?
Social worker: It's not for us to determine where they go.
Psychologist: That's right. The court makes the final ruling—whether he stays here, goes to jail or whatever.

Through conversation, such as that just presented, teams constructed definition of their work as professional discovery and not judicial decision-making. Nonetheless, teams were frequently observed carefully constructing their diagnostic language in terms of what they thought the court needed to hear so that a particular recommendation would be accepted. For instance, one team thought that a particular patient could benefit from staying for further treatment even though he was not believed to be a "psychopathic offender." This team decided to call him a psychopathic offender to obtain treatment for him, although clinically they agreed that this label was inappropriate. Another team thought that a patient was truly a "psychopathic offender," but believed that such persons cannot be treated. They thought that it would be wasteful to hold such an individual in a maximum security hospital when his "psychopathy" could as easily "burn out" in a restricted penal setting. On this basis, they withheld the label "psychopathic offender" and simply recommended that the individual no longer needed the special custody and care of the maximum security setting at Lima.

The careful wording of reports and evaluation statements to secure desired legal outcomes suggests that teams were adjudicating as much as they were discovering psychiatric realities. On the surface this appears to contradict the psychiatric professionals' definitions of themselves as neutral interpreters of data who render expert opinions but do not structure legal decisions. Teams protected themselves from perceiving this contradiction by reinterpreting possible inconsistencies in terms of other "facts" that preserved the "discovery" aspects of their work. For instance, the team that classified a patient as a psychopath in order to get treatment for him introduced a technical distinction between legal and psychiatric psychopathy. Although the label was psychiatrically untrue, the team suggested that it was legally acceptable. As one psychiatrist put it: "In the psychiatric-psychological sense [this] is a little different than it is in the legal sense." Hence the team could give a patient a label that was psychiatrically invalid without explicitly recognizing that they were playing with terminology in order to expedite a particular legal adjudication. It was suggested that "legally" this was their only alternative.

The use of psychiatrically untrue but legally acceptable labels produced legal outcomes compatible with clinical opinions about the need for treatment. In the long run, however, this practice creates two additional problems. First, it places an "untrue" label on a particular patient, a label that then becomes an official part of his diagnostic record. Second, the practice is highly unstandardized. Not all teams used "untrue" labels to get what they wanted; some teams simply avoided imposing any label. One team was concerned that if a patient were called a psychopath, he would have to remain incarcerated. A member of the team said: "I think we could simply waive the psychopathic offender bit and not even say he's recovered or not, just go on and say he doesn't need care, custody, et cetera." This team may include a certain diagnostic term and another may not, but either way there is no telling whether the team thought the term was clinically valid. In reading final reports, it is impossible to discern what a team really had in mind.

Liberal or "Reform-Oriented" Work

Patient-reviewers viewed Lima State Hospital in generally negative terms. Indeed, the public image of this maximum security institution was formed by reports of abuse and neglect. In 1971 the *Cleveland Plain Dealer* condemned the hospital as "a chamber of horrors" because of reports of violence against patients. Against this unfavorable assessment of the hospital as a whole, members spoke of their own work in reformist terms. They frequently expressed the opinion that many Lima patients did not really belong there. They believed that their work would help to release such persons. Moreover, they generally felt that their assessments of patients were liberal or even lenient and that only the most dramatic or overwhelming evidence prompted recommendations for continued maximum security.

Excerpt 2. From Psychiatrist Interview

We didn't recommend many (for) maximum security or dangerousness. . . . Generally we gave, kind of gave, people a chance if they had a fairly reasonable explanation of things and seemed to know where they were going and where they were heading, had some organization to things. Unless the evidence was overwhelmingly against them. If anything, we tended to be more lenient than restrictive. . . . We recommended a lot of them, didn't have to be there. A great percentage. At least 75 percent of them.

"Protecting the Community"

Although members generally saw their work as part of a liberal reform effort, they also thought they were protecting society from potentially harmful criminals. While they believed that many patients had been previously misclassified, they also believed that a sizable portion of the hospital population represented a genuine danger to the public. When the members believed that they had discovered such persons, they had no qualms about recommending confinement. As one member put it, "There are those I would lock up for thirty years at age sixteen."

The psychiatric teams thus assumed that certain patients were clearly dangerous and needed to be isolated from the community. Moreover, dangerous people were perceived to fall into two general categories: those whose "mental disturbances" prevented them from following society's rules and those who had not internalized society's rules in the first place. The first group would simply be labeled "dangerous." The second were considered "psychopathic offenders." For our purposes we shall refer to the first group as characterized by "psychiatric dangerousness" and the second by "psychopathic dangerousness." The criteria by which teams "discovered" each type are discussed below.

Reliance on Life-Threatening Behaviors, Histories of Violence, Assessment of Personal Control, and Certain Idiosyncratic Themes

In considering dangerousness, review teams were instructed to determine whether a patient was extremely likely to do immediate harm to self or others. Several assumptions added specificity to this criterion. The first of these assumptions narrowed the definition of harm. Only behaviors that were considered as "harmful to life" were assumed to be dangerous.

Excerpt 3. From Psychologist Interview

Dangerousness is danger to life. . . . My personal definition of snatching a purse or you know maybe minor physical hurt—I would not consider that real dangerousness. That could happen if a person loses his temper. But when the life is threatened or a very serious physical injury, I would consider that dangerous. Even, I think, in my definition, probably raping I would not consider that very dangerous. Its bad, but I don't consider this dangerous to life.

The restriction of the idea of dangerousness to life-threatening behaviors was typical of the definitions of nearly all team members. Several mentioned forcible rape, along with murder, as an example of dangerous behaviors. Most commonly, however, members believed that sexual assaults that were not accompanied by serious physical injury were not to be categorized as dangerous. This assumption is revealed in the following final evaluation statements. In noting this definitional restriction, it should be remembered that most "sex offenders" were hospitalized as "sexual psychopaths" and (when believed dangerous) could be retained in a maximum security setting by stating that they were still in need of treatment in the hospital's special psychopath unit. In other words, such "psychopathically dangerous" individuals could be retained without being technically designated as dangerous.

Excerpt 4. From Final Evaluation Report

He is considered to have the capability for repeating, almost immediately, the sexual offenses for which he was charged [sexual molestation of young girls]. But he is not considered to be dangerously assaultive, in that it is not felt that he would be likely to kill. It is therefore the opinion of this examining team that this patient is not in need of continued hospitalization in a maximum security facility.

Excerpt 5. From Final Evaluation Report

Even though he does not present immediate danger either to himself or to others, there is a possibility that . . . he may act out violently, especially if provoked and/or in a situation of some seductive maneuver by a member of the female sex. There was some evidence in his record that the patient allegedly molested some female patients while in Dayton State Hospital.

A second assumption about dangerousness involved the criteria teams used to recognize the likelihood for inflicting immediate harm. In nearly all cases, a past history of violence was an assumed prerequisite for viewing a patient as dangerous.

Excerpt 6. From Social Worker Interview

In terms of what occurred between the three of us, I think it's accurate to say that a person would have had to act in a violent fashion, where he would have had to physically harm someone for us to think of him in terms of being dangerous. If that hadn't happened in the past we didn't blame him as such.

A past history of violence was generally constructed from a survey of a patient's record. Team members cited a number of elements within that record that were routinely examined for signs of dangerousness. These included the description of criminal offenses, the record of fights or assaultive incidents within the hospital, and the record of times that a patient was placed in seclusion or in restraint. Also considered was a noted shift in a patient's behavior resulting from shifts in medication.

The prerequisite of a history of violent behavior was modified by two considerations. First, most teams assigned more significance to recent violence than to occurrences in the distant past. Just how distant that past had to be was a judgment that varied across teams and between patients. One team considered that a previous manslaughter incident was unimportant because for the last twenty years the patient had manifested no violence. Another used a ten-year period as a yardstick; still another thought that a patient's ward behavior for the previous two years was the best indicator of potential dangerousness.

A second qualifier to the criterion of past violence occurred in cases where teams noted the presence of "dangerous delusions." Such delusions were most frequently said to represent paranoid constructions in which patients had much self-investment. It was believed that patients who manifested these psychotic symptoms were likely to act out violently to defend their rigid worlds of "unreality." As indicated in the following excerpt, such delusions were often assumed to be predictive of dangerousness despite the absence of any history of violent acts.

Excerpt 7. From Final Evaluation Report

She believes that the Mafia, as well as her mother, brother, and sister-in-law are out to kill her by the use of odorless and tasteless poison. Indeed, she states that these people have gotten to the attendants who then tried to kill her by overdosing her on medicine. . . .

In summary, [the patient] is actively delusional at this time and the previous diagnosis of schizophrenia, paranoid type, still holds. . . . In reference to the question of dangerousness to others, [the patient] has never been assaultive to anyone although she is often argumentative. . . . However, the investment of her delusional system is seen as so great that she might strike out at anybody who tries to disrupt it. . . . This is a mentally ill woman [paranoid schizophrenia] who has the potential of being dangerous to others. It is suggested that she be retained in Lima.

"Recency" and "dangerous delusions" thus modify recorded past violence as a criterion for predicting dangerousness. In general, past violence was treated as a necessary but not sufficient condition in the determination of dangerousness.

Teams also made a fourth assumption: that the truly dangerous individual would reveal his "lack of control" or "lack of ego strength" in the course of an interview. Of course, the manifestation of what was often called "uncontrolled impulsivity" could be inferred from a record of repeated violent offenses. In fact, one team frequently appeared to rely almost exclusively on the past record, even in cases where patients appeared to be presently cooperative and intact and had not evidenced violent or disruptive behaviors for an extended period. Most teams, however, recognized that records were occasionally incomplete or inaccurate and that they gave only an abstract account of incidents that sometimes originated in social situations. Teams thus relied on patients' own explanations for their violence as key elements in assessing the likelihood of immediate dangerousness. The following excerpt describes the process of comparing the patient's own account with the record of what he had done.

Excerpt 8. From Social Worker Interview

We looked at past behaviors. We looked at what it was he did that was called dangerous. . . . Then [in the interview] we asked the patient direct questions about possible harm he's done to himself or others, and if he ever thought about anything like this. . . . How does the person handle it when he gets angry; what does he do; what thoughts and fantasies does he have; what were the circumstances if he did strike out at someone? We always got the patient's point of view on the past behavior.

The assessment of a patient's self-control was assumed to be the central element in an interview to determine dangerousness. In the stress of rapid questioning about past and future violence, it was believed that patients would reveal the degree to which they were in control of any aggressive impulses. Often, teams applied deliberate pressure and provocation through an aggressive interview technique referred to as "stressing." As one psychiatrist indicated, this technique is believed to uncover whether "the individual is so mentally affected that he cannot use restraints." The assumed importance of this aspect of interviewing is documented in the following quotations excerpted from team member interviews.

Excerpt 9. From Psychiatrist Interview

. . . the thing is . . . the amount of control they have in the interview. . . . We did stress them. We thought that was definitely necessary. We guys would shoot questions from the side and occasionally some buts, you know, a few of the fellows would jump up and, you know, some of the crazier ones would go: "I know karate, and you better watch it. I can kill."

The three assumptions discussed so far (that dangerousness meant life threatening behavior, that dangerousness required a past history of violence, and that dangerousness is revealed in the stress of interviewing) were common to each of the review teams. Teams did differ in making more specialized or idiosyncratic assumptions. As already mentioned, one team appeared to place a greater emphasis on the past record. Another team focused more on a patient's ability to express insight into past deeds of violence. Another paid more attention to a patient's verbalization of his or her dreams and fantasies. Another believed the results of psychological testing were very helpful and complained that these were not uniformly available for all patients. Still another team paid considerable attention to signs of dangerousness that it believed to be present in a patient's "repressed anger." According to that team's psychologist, a patient who "could not express anger" was assumed to be "potentially dangerous and explosive." This member cited a case in which the team asked a patient "what it felt like to be a bastard." The patient's passive, nonemotive response ("I don't like it") was assumed to be a cue that anger and potential violence were simmering within. This assumption was also expressed by another member of the same review team, who stated that "I have a feeling if people, if they lash out with very, very little provocation that there must be so much anger that they are likely to murder somebody or kill somebody, or do very real harm."

Another rather idiosyncratic approach to the diagnosis of dangerousness was expressed by one psychiatrist in the following excerpt.

Excerpt 10. From Psychiatrist Interview

I have a feeling we pretty much adhered to our own concept of what we thought would be dangerous. I think we thought in terms of how likely is this man to do something very violent almost immediately after he's turned loose. And another criteria we used was "How would I feel having this man as my next-door neighbor?"

This approach was not common to all teams, but it demonstrates the significance of team members' operating definitions of dangerousness.

Reliance on "Excuse-Making" and
"Rationalizing" Behaviors

A history of life-threatening behaviors was not a necessary criterion in assessing "psychopathic dangerousness." Nonetheless, psychopathic individuals were frequently viewed as even more dangerous than those who had in fact murdered or perpetrated violent assaults in the past. It was reasoned that there was "no telling" what these individuals, without the guidance of a social conscience, would do. They were characterized by one team as "a bunch of scary boys" and by another as "lacking the very quality of humanness." They were generally viewed as "manipulators" and "con artists" who were concerned only with themselves, and from whom society definitely needed protection. Whereas team members relied on cues concerning "lack of control" during interviews to predict dangerousness, signs of "excuse-making" and "rationalizing" were viewed as the most important indicators of the "psychopathic offender." Once diagnosed, custodial recommendations were made to protect society from these persons whom one member described "as more dangerous and definitely with a more guarded prognosis."[13]

Difficult Predictions About the Need for Maximum Security

For most reviewers, predictions about who should remain confined in a maximum security environment were seen as the most difficult type of psychiatric assessment. When there was disagreement among team members, it arose in cases of assessing dangerousness or need for confinement. Assessments of such matters as "mental illness" or "incompetency to stand trial" were viewed as "easy" by comparison. According to one psychologist, a prediction regarding "extreme likelihood of immediate danger" was a "tough point because it was a situational diagnosis." In the words of another clinician, recommendations about the need for maximum security were difficult because "very often a patient described as potentially dangerous [in the record] did not impress us as such during the interview." At other times teams believed that patients were potentially more dangerous than the record suggested. This, too, was said to make predictions more difficult.

Excerpt 11. From Social Worker Interview

Dangerousness, I think, is a word that covers all kinds of grey matter. Depending on certain acts, we really are in the dark as to what kind of history defines dangerousness. In a lot of cases there was very little to document that a guy was dangerous. Now he may have been much more dangerous than what was in the record. In a few cases we found, for example, a newspaper clipping, which kind of clarified why the guy was at Lima State. In those cases you had a piece of journalism which in some ways informed you a lot better than the admission note or the psychiatric history of the guy.

Not all members thought that predictions regarding dangerousness and the need for maximum security were difficult. Some clinicians appeared ready to let a past record "speak for itself." One psychiatrist stated, "Our team found no difficulty in determining dangerousness. Dangerousness was seen in the record, by looking at past performances." According to another, "the patient himself has determined the degree of dangerousness through a history of repeated acts." In general, however, most team members did believe that their predictive tasks were difficult. This difficulty was summed up by a psychiatrist who stated: "I don't think we were able to spell out what exactly they mean by dangerousness. I think that's so difficult."

Confidence in the Accuracy of Predictions

Despite the perceived difficulty of their task, twenty-six of thirty-two clinicians questioned stated that they were confident of the accuracy of their predictions concerning dangerousness and the need for maximum security. Indeed, eleven stated that they were "very confident." The few who were unsure cited knowledge of research and doubts about the accuracy of past records as reasons for being less confident. On the other hand, those who were confident generally trusted both official reports and their own clinical skills. The fact that other team members shared in the same recommendations was also frequently cited as a basis for members' confidence.

Excerpt 12. From Psychiatrist Interview

Yeah, I think we felt confident. . . . We all felt, none of us were new at this, all of us had many years of experience, so that we felt that we could make a diagnosis as well as anybody. And so none of us felt at all backward or had any feelings of serious inferiority, feelings about our capacity to make it. And, as I said, we were able to check each other, support each other, as needed in our decision making. So when we got through, when we came upon a decision, we felt fairly comfortable.

Images of Deviance Produced by the Predictive Review Teams

Review teams were ordered to make predictions about patients' future behaviors and future needs for confinement. In doing so, they produced particular images of dangerous deviants and the way they can best be controlled. These images have obvious implications for the operation of the criminal justice system. They are summarized in the following observations.

Individualistic Explanations for Deviant Behavior

Review teams did not simply categorize patients: They provided them with clinical identities that "explained" (or at least told a story about) why they were dangerous and in need of maximum security confinement or why they might be safely released as harmless. A full discussion of the various interactional strategies through which diagnosticians arrived at identities for patients is beyond the scope of this chapter. Suffice it to say that in reviewing patients' past records, in inducing patients to talk about their "own" problems, and in collectively arriving at formulations of patients' psychological conditions, teams worked hard at fitting patients into individualized theories of deviance.[14] Teams searched extensively and negotiated constantly for the traumatic event, the distorted fantasy, the disrupted relationship that produced an image of the patient. This psychiatric accounting was often constructed after a team had already arrived at its conclusion about a patient. Sometimes knowledge of the past record or a brief "first impression" of the patient was enough to generate explanatory accounts. Much theorizing about a patient's deviant identity took place after a "gut-level" decision by clinicians about his disposition. The theorizing was "reconstructed logic" explaining why clinicians thought what they thought after they thought it.

Teams' early summary judgments about patients are typically illustrated in the following excerpts. These conversations occurred before teams interviewed patients. In such instances, interviews and post-interview discussions are designed to arrive at conclusions about a patient's real identity.[15]

Excerpt 13. From Transcript of Patient Review. (The team is trying to decide whether the patient is a "psychopathic offender" and needs continued custody and care in maximum security.)

Psychologist: The record started when he was thirteen. He's only twenty-two. Nowhere near burning out yet. What else does he have? Does it say? Breaking and entering, that kind of bit?

Psychiatrist: He served time. . . .

Psychologist: He's been around a couple of them. . . .

Psychiatrist: Now most of these people also have in their records . . . a history of broken homes, trouble beginning when they're kids.

Social Worker: It says that he took this with a lesser charge.

Psychologist: What was the first charge?

Social Worker: The original charge was kidnapping. . . . He committed this offense right after he came off parole.

Psychologist: Yeah.

Psychiatrist: Yeah, two days later, I think. . . . He timed it so he wouldn't break parole.

Psychologist: Another stone.

Social Worker: (laugh) Who do you say? He's going to be stoned in the interview.

Psychologist: Stone cold psychopath. [Team then digresses for a few exchanges, making comparisons between psychopaths and other patients. The psychiatrist then "refocuses" the conversation to the topic of patient 421.]

Psychiatrist: Well, I hate to admit this, but my mind is made up on these people even before we see them.

Psychologist: Well, there is wh . . . we do have to, its a matter of degree here.
Social Worker: Its a matter of degree in terms of whether they stay here now or go back to court right away.
Psychiatrist: Yeah.
Psychologist: Well, I'll admit I'm a little prejudiced, but I'm going to withhold my judgment. Basically what this guy is—what twenty-two years of age. Its not just that he's into it. He's a psychopathic offender and he should stay here a longer time. Well, I don't know. . . . Twenty is just a bad age to be working on these guys.
Social Worker: Yeah, they haven't learned.
Psychologist: The twenties is the worst decade to be a psychopath.

In the previous excerpt, such things as a patient's age, the timing of his last offense, and the repetitive nature of offenses are used to construct a theory about the patient as a particular clinical type—the "stone cold psychopath." In the process of interviewing, such theory-building continues. Teams use patients' responses and their own clinical observational skills to document the individual roots of pathology. In the following excerpt, a psychologist "explains" the meaning of a "rather long look" that a patient gave to a research observer. The researcher believed that the patient was just being inquisitive about what he was writing down. The psychologist, equipped with his special clinical skills and with an emerging theory that the patient's past violence was related to his homosexuality, was able to "see" far more. He was able to ascertain a "certain lack of control."

Excerpt 14. From Transcript of Patient Review

Psychologist: I'm bothered by his inability to remember all these things he has been, or his inability to admit remembering. These things that he's done in the past that are associated with homosexuality, and us just. . . .
Psychiatrist: An arbitrary enough homosexual. . . . I guess he's afraid that we'll decide against him, because he's—uh—homosexual. He feels some persecution about being judged a homosexual. And—uh—when he was talking about who he was attracted to—uh—I forgot the question that preceded it, whether or not you asked if he was homosexual or what. I noticed he gave a rather long look to our observer here, and—uh—I don't think that means anything much more than what we all suspect.
Psychologist: Yeah.
Psychiatrist: But—uh—I think it suggests a certain—uh—lack of control, perhaps—uh—in that—uh—or lack of judgment. [As] if he was trying to cover his homosexuality, which he seemed to be doing.

Two other recurrent methods of "theory-building" during interviews include the "offering of individual motives" through the phrasing of questions and the "offering of explanatory commentary" following a patient's response to some question. Sometimes this explanatory commentary, although it is about the patient (i.e., "Now you can see the paranoid defenses in this type of answer"), is addressed exclusively to other team members. It is as if an aside is being made in a play and the patient cannot hear it. An example of the method of "offering motives" is presented below. The clinician suggests that the patient validate an individualized interpretation of his problems.

Excerpt 15. From Transcript of Patient Review. (In this exchange the clinician is pursuing documentation for his theory regarding the patient's poor self-concept and his exaggerated need to impress others.)

Social Worker: Well, so if you got picked up as many times as the other guys that made you as good as the others?
Patient: Not really.
Social Worker: Well, I mean—uh—sort of a prestige thing—uh—that everybody's doing it, getting arrested and somebody who doesn't might be looked down on?
Patient: Well, it might in a sense. A person that might be tougher than everybody.
Social Worker: Everybody was boasting about getting arrested and thrown in jail and so on, or if it was a stolen car?
Patient: Mmmmm, yes.

Excerpt 16. From Transcript of Patient Review. (In this excerpt team members theorize both through asking questions and through offering explanatory commentaries.)

Psychiatrist: Do you like to tell jokes? Can you think of any jokes?
Patient: I don't really know (pause). I hear a lot of Polack jokes from Mr. _____, one of the attendants.
Psychiatrist: Can you think of one?
Patient: Yeah. I can. You want to hear it? (*laugh*) This is funny. This Polack bought this bird dog and took it out one day and came back and took it out again and one Polack said to the other that if that dog don't fly tomorrow, I'm going to shoot him right on the ground. So much for the Polack joke. Hope none of you are Polish.
Psychologist: Would it matter? How much would it matter?
Patient: Well, I don't want to hurt nobody's feelings.
Psychologist: Well you didn't ask first though. You asked later.
Patient: That's another thing I do. You know, sometimes I say something and stop and think that wasn't a very good thing to say.
Psychologist: Feel embarrassed now? Your ears are turning a little red.
Patient: No, not embarrassed, a little idiotic that you wanted me to tell these jokes. But I guess you're just trying to make me feel comfortable.
Psychologist: No. I'm not trying to make you feel comfortable. People, uh, the kind of jokes that people think or tell or enjoy helps me to know something about them. . . . (*pause*) The joke that you told has

something to do with the way you feel about yourself. The dumb Polack joke. You refer to yourself as a dumb hillbilly?

In post-interview discussions, teams solidify their theorizing about the roots of an individual patient's pathology. Often as soon as a patient leaves the room, team members make statements such as, "Well, it's obvious to me . . ." or "It's pretty clear that the patient is. . . ." Sometimes a final theory awaits negotiations and compromises among team members. In any event, the situational basis for a particular diagnosis is dropped off in the formulation of a final theory about the patient's individual problems. For instance, in the case of the individual whose pathology was indexed by his "dumb Polack" joke, the logic that governed team members' assessments is discarded in favor of a professionalized "reconstructed logic." In discussing a final recommendation, the psychologist inquires of the psychiatrist, "What would you say. Inadequate personality?" The psychiatrist responds: "Why, certainly I would weigh that adult stress reaction. And I would say inept personality. And then the sexual deviation is explaining the act he committed." In the case of the individual theoretically cast as being overdependent on others, the team drew on a previous entry in the patient's record to suggest evidence of "emotional immaturity and group delinquency reaction of adolescence." The "uncontrolled look" by the individual allegedly denying his homosexuality was transformed into a statement that "he shows apparent personality disorder, with paranoid schizoid elements." The diagnosticians succeeded in constructing (or fitting patients into) theories about individual deviance. These theories accompany and justify recommendations for release or retention.

Sustaining the "Impression" that Deviance Can Be
Identified and Managed at the Level of Individual
Psychopathology

In constructing individual theories of deviance, diagnosticians fix the blame for violent, harmful, or dangerous behavior on the psychiatric realities of "psychopathology" of patients. Such practical theorizing preserves the professional identity of psychiatric diagnosticians. It also denigrates patients' attempts to "socially account" for psychiatric problems.

The professional identity of diagnosticians is preserved (or situationally accomplished) through the specialized language and style of their reports about patients. As mentioned previously, the empirical basis for these reports (i.e. the joke, the "long look," the response to a "motive loaded" question) is discarded in favor of abstract professional terminology depicting "syndromes" and "symptoms." This display of professional theorizing and expert language was an important part of team members' interactions with one another. It functioned to sustain in the diagnostic dialogue their identities as experts in what they were doing. Yet, as important as it was to maintain professional appearances before each other, it was equally important to establish the appearance of expertise before the legal audience to which they reported. Feelings were transformed into findings, perceived states of affairs into expert opinions. As illustrated below, displays of uncertainty or confusion were eliminated from final reports.

Excerpt 17. From Transcript of Patient Review. (The team is making its final recommendations. It has spent considerable time trying to make sense out of a patient's jumbled legal record.)

Social Worker: [Dictating the report.] This team is confused and unable to determine the present legal status of. . . .
Psychologist: No. Don't say we're confused, even if we are. . . .
Social Worker: Oh, Okay. What if I say we were unable, from the record, to determine the basis.
Psychologist: Right. It's the legal record that's the problem.

The maintenance of an expert identity requires teams to disguise ambivalence and confusion. It also requires that cautious phrasing be used in cases where teams may, in fact, be skeptical of the predicative consequences implied by their apparently expert pronouncements. The use of such "discretionary vagueness" is explained in the following statement.

Excerpt 18. From Psychiatrist Interview.

If a patient is in the hospital, he is medicated. He's improved and so on, fine. He might act out two or three days later again. But today, if you interview and find no, I'm not saying this individual is dangerous. We never do this. We say he is potentially dangerous, although controlled at this time. You know, you never leave the door that wide open. Not with these cases.

Through the careful use of professional language, psychiatric diagnosticians manage a professional identity of themselves as technically proficient predictors of dangerousness. Theorizing about the individual or psychopathological basis for patients' problems also serves to deny the validity of social accounts for patients' present situations. Specifically, it requires clinicians to discount explanations that may have little to do with "psychiatric reality" but a lot to do with cultural, class, or political reality. For instance, a patient may come from a cultural setting in which much of the world is interpreted through the notions of "fate" or "chance." He may have lived in a lower-class setting in which violence was construed as a "normal" response to personal affronts. He may now live in a setting where his "disruptive behaviors" are frequently provoked by the discriminatory or abusive actions of those "in charge." Actually, most Lima State patients come from, have lived in, and presently dwell in all three such settings. Nonetheless, accounts concerning their behaviors using fatalistic cultural notions, lower-class definitions of violence, or a political analysis of hospital pressures are routinely interpreted as evidence of delusional thinking, denials of responsibility, and paranoid reactions. In this way, attempts to fit patients into theories about psychiatric realities function to obscure the other realities by which patients ordinarily live.

Our suggestion that psychiatric theorizing denigrates social accounts does not imply that diagnosticians never consider cultural, class, or political variables. At various points, clinicians were observed making statements such as "Well, we can't be shocked. We have to consider that this (incest) is more common among these (mountain) people. It doesn't have the same moral meaning." "Boy, I'll tell you. He comes from a part of Cleveland, mmmmm, [where] I'd carry a gun around." "You know, the first-degree murder thing, it was because he killed a white man. If it was a black it would have been different."

At first glance, the statements appear to widen the understanding of a patient's troubles, opening the door to other social accounts for his "deviance." But this is not how such statements are used in practical psychiatric theorizing. These statements can represent a sympathetic viewing of a patient, but they are not allowed to pass as theoretical accounts for personal troubles. They may help a team "see" that the patient is a cooperative and honest person. They will not help explain why the patient did what he did, however. An illustration of this contention is found in the case of a young black male who was paralyzed from the waist down from a shooting incident several years ago. He was charged with carrying a concealed weapon. His parents, who believed he was acting "too wild" and disturbed around the house, reported him to the police. Their testimony in court was apparently a key element in his commitment to Lima State Hospital until he was restored to reason. During the interview, the patient was composed, but he stated that he would probably continue to carry a weapon to protect his property and that he had refused to take his medication because it made him sick.

After the patient left the room, the psychologist discussed signs of paranoid schizophrenia and expressed concern over the patient's intent to carry a gun, his almost "unnatural fear" of someone taking his property, and his "perceived emnity or hostility towards his family." The psychiatrist elaborated upon this, stating: "This is abnormal. You don't carry a knife around to stab someone becauese you feel you'll get stabbed. This man was disturbed." The social worker initially seemed less sure of this line of theorizing. Shouldn't the case be seen in relation to a social-cultural milieu in which gun-carrying would be seen as "normal"? The psychiatrist responded by pointing out that while these broader issues were important, they were really not the patient's problem. His problem was psychiatrically refocused at the individual level. His disturbed behavior at home was the "real" issue. The social worker accepted this "insight" and returned to theorizing about the patient's individualized trouble. Late in the interview, even the social worker theorized entirely at the level of individualistic psychiatric reality. The patient's disturbed behavior was discussed as a form of compensation for his physical disability. Social accountings were discarded in favor of individualized psychiatric explanations.

The preoccupation of psychiatric diagnosticians with individualistic explanations for deviance has definite political implications. As agents of social control, these professionals represent the state's power to hospitalize its citizens involuntarily. By emphasizing the importance of one explanatory framework (psychiatric) to the near exclusion of another (social), psychiatric assessments of dangerousness function to control the acceptability of certain "realities" as well as behaviors. Often this inattention to other than individualistic psychiatric themes seems sociologically naive. In one case a team asked a lower-class male patient what he would do if he were on a public bus and someone came up and started calling him obscene names. The patient stated that it depended on whether the person was a male or a female. If it was a male, he said that the person deserved to get punched. Such an answer is probably to be expected from the perspective of a culture and class, in which the possibility of violence and rigid distinctions between expectations for males and females are taken as commonplace. From the vantage point of psychiatric diagnosticians, however, the situation looked quite different. Team members noted the distinction between males and females "as if" it were evidence of the patient's ambivalence toward women and saw the fact that the event may precipitate violence as indicative that "his judgment remains impulsive."

In another case, a patient's story about being victimized by a "crackpot psychiatrist," by staff discrimination, and by the lack of treatment in Lima State Hospital and at a home for delinquents—which he described as more a jail than a school—were taken as evidence of his need to rationalize and drive to manipulate. One woman's story of sexual abuse at the hospital was taken as evidence of delusions and projections of her homosexual identity to others, although she had previously testified at public hearings about this incident. As the team suggested in formulating its final opinion, "some of this goes on but mostly it's just her delusions."

The preceding examples were presented as illustrations of a prevailing pattern.[16] Potentially plausible cultural, class, and political accounts are struck down in favor of explanations that favor a focus on the individual roots of social deviance. This practice has important implications, not only for the diagnostic fate of individual patients, but for the system of social control as a whole. The present system of criminal justice is, after all, constructed on an individualistic model of deviance. It is the individual offender who is held culpable for violations against the sociolegal order of things. The work of diagnostic professionals reinforces the operation of that system. Their work in "discovering" the individual roots of dangerousness and need for maximum security, and their disregard of cultural, class, and political accounts regarding these matters underscores the belief that violent crimes are best explained in terms of troublesome or pathological individuals. Thus while achieving a sense of expert identity, diagnosticians simultaneously further the interests of the existing mechanisms of social control.

Summary Remarks

The psychiatric assessment of dangerousness and need for maximum security is a political act because through it the state's power is invoked to restrict citizens' freedoms. Insofar as we have observed that diagnosticians favor individualized psychiatric accounts to the exclusion of social explanations for deviance, their acts are political in a second sense as well. They play a "gatekeeping" function whereby a certain version of human reality—that which explains troublesome behavior at the individual or psychopathological level—is rewarded, and other versions—those that explain behavior in terms of cultural, class, or political accounts—are punished. Past, present, or possibly future behaviors are wrenched from their social context. They are interpretively converted by psychiatric diagnosticians into theories of personal pathology. Moreover, the empirical basis for judgments about the psychogenic roots of deviance is transformed or obscured by the use of an abstract professional language. The management of this language helps to secure an expert identity for its users. It also serves to mask essentially moral or political judgments in the logic and rhetoric of psychiatric expertise. The whole process of psychiatric determination of the needs to be confined supports a criminal justice system that emphasizes individuals rather than collectivities as the real perpetrators of violence and harm.

In observing the political implications of the prediction process, it is not suggested that psychiatric diagnosticians consciously victimize anyone, deliberately denigrate other versions of reality, or intentionally participate in the maintenance of a particular system of social control. These things happen. The perspective of the diagnosticians themselves is best characterized by the term "false consciousness." They are sincere in viewing their work as discovery. They appear capable of simultaneously supporting ideals of reform and social control.

Despite the "good" intentions of the psychiatric professionals, however, psychiatric predictions of need for confinement have "bad" consequences and should be abandoned, for such predictions have not proved better than decisions by mere chance. They have produced high rates of false positives as well as depreciating the social realities. Worst of all, they have reinforced an assumption within the criminal justice system that systematically prevents the realization of social justice: the assumption that violent or dangerous behavior can best be explained at the individual or psychogenic level. This assumption reifies an individualistic view of the world while discrediting the conception that human potentials, possibilities, and practices are intricately related to the fates of the collectivities in which they live and find both meaning and existence.[17] Through almost exclusive adherence to this principle, the criminal justice system can isolate violence in the acts of individuals. Ignored are social meanings of such acts. These meanings may vary greatly in terms of self-consciousness or reflective awareness. Certainly the violence of the political terrorist and the violence of the youth defending his "rep" in the street fight or the husband his "masculinity" in the bedroom are not to be equated. Yet each may express the problems of power and privilege or the experience of their absence. The meaning of such violence represents a range of human action considerably wider than the restrictive scope of psychiatric reality.[18]

Let us make a suggestion for a modest improvement in psychiatric predictions. We have argued that decisions about who needs to be confined in maximum security are inherently political. Hence, if these decisions must be made (as they will be in the forseeable future), they should be rendered in a more explicitly political forum such as that of a jury hearing in a formal court setting. We have also argued that psychiatric predictions are not particularly accurate in sorting out dangerous persons or psychopathic individuals; they are expert only in the careful management of their user's professional identities. These careful management practices should be discarded and the work of psychiatric professionals should be displayed as but one input within the context of advocacy and cross-examination. If this is done, the usefulness of psychiatric judgments can be preserved, without treating these judgments as the objective products of expert technologies. Psychiatric professionals can be queried about the bases for their opinions. Decision-makers can be exposed to their inferential logic-in-use as well as their justificatory logic of professional resonstruction.

The suggestion of a juried hearing is based on observations of several of the few cases in which Lima State patients appealed the recommendations set forth by psychiatric review teams. Legal advocates debated the issue of a patient's dangerousness and need for confinement and interrogated the "experts" involved in a decision. In one case the psychiatric team had concluded that a patient was "a creature of pure impulse, with no controls whatsoever, no conscience, and no feelings of remorse or sensibility" and that he was "considered to be immediately dangerous to others and in continued need of hospitalization in a maximum security facility." During the hearing, legal advocates produced evidence that the patient "had not shown aggressiveness or assaultiveness" during his stay at the hospital. Testimony by hospital staff indicated that "the patient could be adequately cared for outside a maximum security institution." In the light of this additional evidence, the court reversed the recommendation of the "experts" and decided that the patient did not need maximum security. The court was informed by more than psychiatric predictions, and rightly so. We conclude that the professional prediction of dangerousness should be replaced by public adjudication. This would ensure that judgments regarding involuntary confinement remain in the explicitly political arena to which they belong.

The institutionalization of mandatory adjudication may devaluate the expertise of psychiatric decision-makers, which will elicit considerable opposition from psychiatric professionals themselves. As Brodsky has observed, the well-versed cross-examiner can create "an 'expert witness' nightmare." While the adversary system "provides a base of common challenge points," it may, for the uncertain witness, precipitate a discrediting experience.[19] Nonetheless, our consistent discovery of inconsistency, disguised as professional caution, indicates that the adversary situation is required for fairness to the individual whose fortunes turn on these professional perceptions.

Throughout this chapter we have been concerned with the processes by which "expert psychiatric knowledge" is assembled about patients and "expert status" accorded to its creators. We have been led to certain moral and political reservations about the present status of psychiatric contributions to decisions about dangerousness. We have concluded that psychiatric knowledge is a well-managed "appearance of objectivity" rather than a set of "objective facts." Its factual authenticity must not be taken for granted. It counts—and counts heavily—in the lives of patients whose psychological and social realities are assessed in terms of their dangerousness and need for maximum security.

Because of the serious consequences of psychiatric decision-making, we believe that the basis for its "authority," and its dependence on a process of negotiated social interaction, should be displayed for public scrutiny. We hope that the presentation of our findings represents a step in this direction. We are confident that the public adjudication of each attempt to confine someone as dangerous (or in need of maximum security) will represent another more permanent advance. This step will realize the spirit of Judge David Bazelon's ruling in the case of *Covington* v. *Cameron,*[20] which stated that it was the court's responsibility to see that psychiatric decision-makers reach "reasoned" and not "unreasonable" conclusions, employ "proper criteria," and "do not overlook anything of substantial relevance." To bring decision-makers out of the mystic shelter of expertise and into the public scrutiny of the courtroom should advance these goals. We conclude by agreeing with Judge Bazelon that "to do less would abandon the interests affected to the absolute power of administrative officials."[21]

Notes

1. Actually, although Lima State Hospital has been traditionally referred to as a hospital for the "criminally insane," only a small proportion of its nearly

700 patients were technically "not guilty by reason of insanity." About one-third of its patients were "mentally ill offenders" transferred from penal settings. Another third were classified as "incompetent" and still waiting to stand trial, while about one-fifth of the patients were "psychopathic offenders," hospitalized under Ohio's version of a "sexual psychopath statute." The remaining patients were split between those "not guilty by reason of insanity," those transferred (as behavior problems) from civil mental hospitals, and those believed to have incurred mental problems while on probation or parole.

2. Other results of this "right to treatment" ruling involved the setting of minimum standards for treatment. For a fuller discussion of this case and others, see Stephen J. Pfohl, *Right to Treatment Litigation: A Consideration of Judicial Intervention Into Mental Health Policy* (Columbus, Ohio: Ohio Division of Mental Health, 1975).

3. Technically, decisions about "dangerousness" (i.e., the extreme likelihood of inflicting immediate harm) and those regarding "psychopathic offenders" (i.e., needing the continued custody and care of Lima State Hospital) were different. The practical consequences, however, were the same: continued confinement. For our present purposes, we are less concerned with what technically embodies a decision than we are with the assumptions and interests of the decision-makers. As such, both categories of decisions about continued confinement will be considered simultaneously.

4. Norval Morris, *The Future of Imprisonment* (Chicago: University of Chicago Press, 1974), pp. 62-63.

5. Pfohl, p. 24.

6. Ernst Wenk, J. Robison, and G. Smith, "Can Violence Be Predicted?" *Crime and Delinquency* 18 (1972): 393-402.

7. Edwin Megargee, "The Prediction of Violence with Psychological Tests," in C. Speilberger (ed.), *Current Topics in Clinical and Community Psychology* (New York: Academic Press, 1970), pp. 98-156.

8. Harry Kozol, R. Boucher, and R. Garofalo, "The Diagnosis and Treatment of Dangerousness," *Crime and Delinquency* (1972): vol. 18:371-392, 1972; Henry Steadman and Joseph Cocozza, *Careers of the Criminally Insane* (Lexington, Mass.: Lexington Books, D.C. Heath, 1974).

9. Actually, rates are usually considerably lower. The "maximum rate" referred to here would entail the retention of all "criminally insane" or "forensic" patients under age fifty, while still incurring a 2:1 ratio of false positive predictions (see Steadman and Cocozza). Other studies (such as Wenk, Robison, and Smith) have found the false prediction rate to be as high as 95 percent.

10. Bruce J. Ennis and Thomas R. Litwack, "Psychiatry and the Presumption of Expertise: Flipping the Coins in the Courtroom," *California Law Review* 62 (May 1974): 693-752.

11. Alan Dershowitz, "Psychiatrists' Power in Civil Commitment," *Psychology Today* 2 (February 1969): 47.

12. Morris, p. 63.

13. In addition to their belief that "psychopathic offenders" were among the most dangerous of patients, some teams also believed that they were "untreatable." Their model for understanding these persons assumed that psychopaths cannot learn from experience and that their antisocial personalities can "burn out" only with age. As such, some psychopathic offenders were recommended for release from a maximum security "treatment" setting and transfer to a penal setting where they simply pass time (something that was assumed to be the only effective solution for their "psychopathy"). Other teams that assumed that psychopaths could be treated recommended that similar individuals be kept in the maximum security hospital where they truly belonged.

14. Teams generally searched for evidence to confirm "theories" that were being developed about patients, but this does not mean that patients had no impact on the outcomes of psychiatric decisions. Interviews with selected patients convinced us that patients often tried to manage a particular identity in front of team members. Sometimes patients' "resistance" clearly altered the direction of diagnosticians theorizing. So did the occasional resistance of team members to each other. In such cases, where theories were modified or compromised, teams appeared to display an additional show of reconstructed logic, in demonstrating wither "that's what we were saying all along anyway" or "it's only different because of 'new evidence,' not better theorizing."

15. Teams all worked to construct "individualized theories" during their final post-interview discussions. Not all teams "theorized" to the same extent in reviewing records and interviewing patients. For instance, three of eleven teams observed showed little evidence of "theory construction" before talking with patients. Two of these had actually decided not to review records until after talking with patients. Only two teams out of eleven displayed no evidence of theorizing about patients in their actual interviewing procedures.

16. Of the eleven teams observed, only one seemed particularly open to accounts other than the "psychiatric." It should be noted, however, that an occasional display of "sociological" knowledge was employed as a disclaimer in the promotion of more individualized theorizing. For instance, a psychiatric explanation was sometimes prefaced by the lead-in phrase: "Well, of course this does happen and it could be the case, *but. . . .*"

17. The suggestion that human conduct is intricately related to, rather than determined by, the socioeconomic forces that shape the fate of collectivities is quite deliberate. We are here presenting a "critical analysis" that envisions individual actions as restrained, but not caused by infrastructural variables.

18. There is no attempt here to romanticize "proletarian violence." The relation between the meaning of violence for the actor and the experience of

relative powerlessness has been mapped out in numerous investigations. See Lynn Curtis, *Violence, Race, and Culture* (Lexington, Mass.: Lexington Books, D.C. Heath, 1975).

19. Stanley L. Brodsky, *Psychologists in the Criminal Justice System* (Carbondale, Ill.: Admark, 1972), p. 95.

20. See *Covington* v. *Cameron*, 419 F.2d 617 (D.C. Cir. 1969).

21. Bazelon is here excerpted in Jonas Robitscher, "The Right to Treatment: A Social-Legal Approach to the Plight of the State Hospital Patient," *Villanova Law Review*, 18 (November 1972): 19.

The Incapacitation of the Dangerous Offender: A Statistical Experiment

Stephan Van Dine,
Simon Dinitz, and
John P. Conrad

Of the possible benefits of incarceration, the protection of the public from violent crime is receiving considerable speculative attention from social critics. By restraining men disposed to the commission of violence, it is argued, the streets will become safer for as long as the restraint is in effect. Wilson (1975) and van den Haag (1975) have both made this point vigorously, referring to the landmark cohort study of Wolfgang, Figlio, and Sellin (1972) and the less well-known work of Shlomo and Reuel Shinnar (1975). This argument has been persuasive in many quarters, leading to the advocacy of a "hard line" in sentencing adult offenders convicted of crimes aginst the person. The call for long and mandatory sentences for these offenders is increasingly insistent.

Recent attempts to provide empirical evidence in support of an incapacitation policy have led to conflicting conclusions. In a marginal reference to the measurement of the incapacitation effect of punishment, Ehrlich (1973) suggested that less than 10 percent of the impact of imprisonment on the crime rate could be attributed to the restraint of offenders. Ehrlich's analysis included all seven index offenses and was based on a regression model for the study of the effects of deterrence; he did not derive a more specific value for incapacitation as it related to the four violent index crimes.

Clarke (1974) used data produced by the Philadelphia Birth Cohort study (Wolfgang et al. 1972) to estimate the extent to which crime would have increased if no juvenile had been confined. He computed a yearly average of index crimes committed by each chronic juvenile recidivist, and multiplied that average by the number of serious offenders incarcerated each year. The result is an increase of 5 to 15 percent in crime committed by the Wolfgang 1945 Birth Cohort; a similar increase in crime for all juveniles would have been reflected in an increase of 1 to 4 percent in reported crimes in Philadelphia.

Relying principally on California data, Greenberg (1975) estimated that each one-year reduction in average sentence length would result in increases in the index crime rates of from 1.2 to 8.0 percent. This study rests on debatable

This chapter is a revised version of an article by the same title that appeared in the January 1977 issue of the *Journal of Research in Crime and Delinquency.* (Vol. 14, No. 1, pp. 22-34.) Reprinted by permission.

We would like to thank Robert Backoff, and Jan Palmer, both of The Ohio State University, and John Salimbene, of the Franklin County (Ohio) Prosecutor's Office for their helpful comments on earlier drafts of this essay.

assumptions. Greenberg estimates that the true figure for return to prison with convictions for new crimes during the first year after release will approximate 8 percent, a much lower figure than usually suggested. The discrepancy is attributable to the exclusion of technical parole violations. Greenberg finally arrives at an average rate of index crimes committed by recidivists within a range of 0.5 to 4.3 crimes per recidivist per year. His calculation also rests on the dubious assumption that the average duration of a criminal career is five years, arguing that the higher averages usually accepted underrepresent one-crime offenders. He also inflates the crime rates reported in the Uniform Crime Reports by a multiplier derived from victimization studies. Greenberg's analysis concludes with two important and credible speculations; first, the low level of incapacitation that he infers from the data is attributable in part to the low rate of commission of serious crime by parolees. His second speculation points to the low rate of incarceration for index crimes. Obviously, if a more severe policy of restraint were applied, the incapacitative effects of imprisonment would substantially increase. Thus Clarke and Greenberg both conclude that incapacitation, as presently administered, has a relatively modest impact on the crime rate. Ehrlich's projections would also fall within this range unless the reported violent crime rate were twice as high without the deterrent effect of punishment as at present.

The study by Shlomo and Reuel Shinnar (1975) approaches the problem from a different perspective and set of assumptions. Using data from the Uniform Crime Reports, they attempt to arrive at an estimate of the amount of crime which might be prevented by a much more severe sentencing policy. They estimate that the average number of crimes committed in the course of a criminal career is about 25 and that recidivists constitute 16 percent of the criminal population but commit about 90 percent of the crimes. The significant estimate derived from this analysis is that the career criminal commits six to fourteen offenses per year while getting caught once. Therefore the Shinnars boldly project that mandatory sentences, five years for violent index crimes and three years for burglary, could reduce the incidence of these crimes by 80 percent.

The studies discussed here are applications of various explanatory models to existing statistics of crime and delinquency. The investigation which will be described in this chapter attempts to fill an empirical gap. The basic question that we shall address is: How many actual offenses might have been prevented by sentencing policies designed for the purpose of incapacitating the dangerous offender? In the next section, we shall set forth the methodology by which we arrive at an estimate based on an extensive case-by-case review of the histories of all violent offenders indicted in the Court of Common Pleas for Franklin County (Columbus), Ohio during the year 1973.

Methodology

Our fundamental question cannot be answered without addressing subsidiary problems. The two primary issues can be formulated as follows:

1. How much violent crime will be prevented by an explicit policy of sentencing for incapacitation?
2. How long must sentences be if incapacitation is to make a significant impact on the violent crime rates?

Breaking these questions down to produce answers relevant to policy, we tried to design a study that would settle, so far as possible, the specific issues confronting the legislature in establishing sentencing limits and the courts in establishing actual terms of custodial confinement for offenders to be sentenced. We need to know the specific consequences of varying incapacitation policies on the incidence of homicide, robbery, aggravated assault, and forcible rape. How many of these crimes would be prevented by the restraint of repetitively violent criminals for periods of three or five years? Of violators with previous histories of nonviolent offenses only? Of those under some specific age level reserved for the juvenile court? In short, what can the criminal histories of actual offenders tell us about the optimal sentencing policies if the reduction of violent crime is to be the object of a policy of incapacitation?

The 1973 Indictment and Conviction File

To address these and related questions, we collected all recorded data on every person charged with each of the violent crimes enumerated above in Franklin County (Columbus), Ohio in 1973.[1] In 1973, 364 adults were arrested and charged with one or more murders and manslaughters, robberies, aggravated assaults, and violent sex offenses. Of these 364 persons, 14 were charged with violent crimes committed while in prison or as escapees from a penal institution. These 14 cases were eliminated from the universe of eligible subjects. Also excluded were 8 subjects for whom no previous criminal histories could be found in the files of the Columbus Police Department, the Franklin County Sheriff's Department, the Ohio Bureau of Criminal Identification, the F.B.I., or the Ohio Department of Rehabilitation and Corrections. Elimination of the 14 prison inmates and escapees and the 8 persons with missing files reduced the cohort to 342 subjects.

The 342 remaining individuals met the following criteria. All were adults or juveniles bound over and charged as adults. All had been indicted or arraigned for one of the major personal crimes. All were listed by the Franklin County Prosecutor as "disposed of" (cases completed) during the 1973 calendar year. The prosecutor "disposes of" a person charged with a crime in one of three ways: a plea of *nolle prosequi* is entered, usually because the prosecutor lacks sufficient evidence; the case proceeds to trial and the defendant is acquitted; or the defendant pleads guilty or is so found in the trial. A case is not considered complete until the immediate appeals are concluded.

Of our cohort of 342 Franklin County violent offenders in 1973, 166 were found guilty as charged. The remainder, 176 cases, were distributed between the two-thirds who were released on writs of *nolle prosequi* and "no bills," and the other third, who, after plea-bargaining, pled guilty to a lesser offense. We have divided our cohort accordingly into two groups, those who were found guilty as charged, and those who were indicted but not convicted on the violent crime charge. Our analysis separates these two groups, as will be seen in the tables we present.

Nevertheless, it is essential to understand that our basic assumption holds that *all subjects in the cohort, whether found guilty or not of the crimes with which they were charged, did in fact commit all the crimes for which they were arrested.* Thus a man who was arrested for fourteen robberies but tried and convicted on only three, is assumed, for the purpose of this study, to have committed all fourteen. If he had been subjected to a mandatory sentence on his last previous conviction of a felony, the resulting incapacitation would be counted as preventing all fourteen offenses. This assumption deliberately overstates the effectiveness of an incapacitation policy. We are interested here in exploring the maximum potential of imprisonment in the prevention of crime; this assumption yields a maximum estimate of the effectivenes of adult incapacitation policies, as far as our data will let us go. To develop a minimum estimate of effectiveness, we compare convictions prevented to the number of crimes committed.

The uses of official records have limitations well known to criminologists. It would have been desirable to complete our analysis by presenting the influence of the variables of socioeconomic status, educational level, employment histories, and other items of social differentiation, but the only uniform social information available identified those under study by age and race.

To test the effectiveness of incapacitation, we needed to determine how many of the 1973 offenses would have been prevented if an incapacitating sentence had been imposed at the last previous conviction. We tested five hypothetical sentencing policies, as follows:

Sentencing Option I: Assume that on any felony conviction, whether violent or not, a five-year net mandatory prison term was imposed.

Sentencing Option II: Assume that on any felony conviction after the first (second and following), whether violent or not, a five-year net mandatory prison term was imposed. On the first conviction the penalty structure continues as under present law.

Sentencing Option III: Assume that on any felony conviction after the second (third and following), whether violent or not, a five-year net mandatory prison term was imposed. On the first two convictions the penalty structure continues as under present law.

Sentencing Option IV: Assume that on any felony conviction, whether violent or not, a three-year net mandatory prison term was imposed.

Sentencing Option V: Assume that on any first violent felony conviction, a five-year net mandatory prison term was imposed. For any subsequent violent or nonviolent felony by the same offender, a five-year net mandatory prison term was imposed. For offenders convicted of only nonviolent felonies, the penalty structure continues as under present law.

The adult histories of the 342 arrested and charged 1973 violent offenders were examined to obtain the following information:

1. Did they have any previous felony conviction?
2. Were any such convictions for prior violent crimes?
3. When was the last felony conviction recorded prior to the 1973 conviction?
4. Would the imposition of a three- or five-year sentence for the earlier violation have prevented the 1973 offense? Would any of the 342 have been in prison under a stiffer earlier sentence and consequently been incapable of the 1973 murder/manslaughter, robbery, aggravated assault or violent sex offense?

Each case in the cohort was reviewed to provide an answer to each of these questions. In addition to arrest and court records, the F.B.I. arrest histories were also examined and coded. In this way each criminal career represented in the sample could be charted to determine the effect of a mandatory sentence of the length called for in each option for each offender meeting the criteria of the options under evaluation.

Results

Table 6-1 presents our cohort in a distribution of the offenses for which they were indicted, the number of crimes with which they were charged, and the number of crimes charged per defendant. Robbery is by far the most frequent crime, and although this offense may be brutally violent, it may also be without violence inflicted or intended. Note also that if the robberies included under the separate heading of multiple offense category are combined with the robbery category, the total number of robbers would be 168, nearly half our sample. By

Table 6-1

Distribution of Cohort by Crime of Indictment, Numbers of Crimes, and Number of Crimes per Indictee

	Persons Indicted	Crimes Charged, by Categories of Persons Indicted	Charges/Person
Murder/manslaughter	36	45	1.2
Robbery	128	269	2.1
Sex offenses (violent)	79	111	1.4
Assault	49	66	1.3
Multiple offense (two of the above)	50[a]	147[b]	2.9
Total	342	638	1.9

[a]Of the 50 persons, 22 were charged with robbery-assault offenses, 12 with robbery-sex offenses, 6 with murder/manslaughter-robbery offenses, 6 with murder/manslaughter-assault offenses, 3 with assault-sex offenses, and 1 with murder/manslaughter-sex offenses.

[b]The 50 persons charged with multiple offenses generated 147 charges, of which there were 17 murder charges, 55 robbery charges, 32 sex offenses, and 43 assault offenses.

the nature of this multiple offense category group, the robbers included in it must be presumed to be especially dangerous.

Attrition of the indictment sample is evident in table 6-2, which shows that only 166, or 48 percent, of the 342 persons indicted were convicted on violent charges for which they were indicted. Plea bargaining played an important role. Most of those convicted of a violent offense were convicted of fewer counts than the number for which they were indicted. Reduction of charges was quantitative as well as qualitative; it was not uncommon to find that eleven of fourteen robbery counts, for example, were dismissed, leaving three counts for the actual conviction. A robbery and rape in the indictment resulted in a rape conviction. As previously indicated where charges were dismissed in this manner, we counted them as actual offenses that might have been prevented by a policy of incapacitation.

As indicated in table 6-3, the 342 original members of the cohort were responsible for 638 offenses, which were cleared by their arrest. The 166 men who were convicted cleared only 231 offenses. These figures compare with the 2892 violent index offenses reported in Franklin County in the 1973 *Uniform Crime Reports*. At the arrest level, the 638 charges represent 22.1-percent clearance on the reported violent crimes, but at the conviction level only 8.0 percent of these crimes finally resulted in a conviction. There was the usual variation in clearance rates. Clearance by arrest for murder/manslaughter amounted to 95.4 percent and by conviction to 52.3 percent; this compares with national clearances for these crimes for 1973 of 81.0 percent and 26.4 percent respectively. Clearance rates for Franklin County aggravated assaults were 11.5

Table 6-2

Distribution of Cohort by Crime of Conviction, Number of Convictions, and Number of Conviction-Counts per Offender

	Persons Convicted	Conviction-Counts	Conviction-Counts per Offender
Murder/manslaughter	18	20	1.1
Robbery	77	100	1.3
Sex offenses (violent)	23	24	1.0
Assault	28	30	1.1
Multiple offense (two of the above)	20[a]	57[b]	2.8
Total	166	231	1.4

[a]Of the twenty persons with multiple offenses, six each were convicted for robbery-assault offenses and with murder/manslaughter-assault offenses, five for murder/manslaughter-robbery offenses, and one offender for each of three combinations: murder/manslaughter-sex offenses, robbery-sex offenses, assault-sex offenses.

[b]The twenty offenders convicted on multiple offenses generated fifty-seven conviction-counts, of which there were fourteen murder conviction-counts, twenty robbery conviction-counts, five sex offense conviction-counts, and eighteen assault conviction-counts.

percent by arrest and 5.1 percent by conviction. Although 43.9 percent of the violent sex offenses were cleared by arrest, only 8.9 percent resulted in convictions, which probably reflects the difficulty in prosecuting such cases to a conclusion.

The Frequency of Prior Felony Convictions

Of our 342 cohort members, only 107 had prior felony convictions. Table 6-4 indicates the offense record of the 342 subjects. It is important to note that the average interval between the 1973 offense and the immediately previous felony conviction was 5.56 years, although the median interval was 3.6 years. Examining the interval between convictions of the 107 recidivists, we found that an incapacitation period of three years would have prevented, at the most, only 42.4 percent of these persons from committing their 1973 offenses. With a five-year incapacitation, 63.7 percent of the recidivists might have been prevented from the commission of the 1973 violent offenses.

The Tests of Incapacitation

Our most severe sentencing option, designated here as Option I, provides that every convicted felon, regardless of the nature of the offense, will receive a

Table 6-3
Total Recorded Violent Offenses and Violent Offenses Cleared, Franklin County, 1973

	Reported Violent UCR Crimes Franklin County, 1973[a]	Cleared by Arrest		Cleared by by Conviction	
		N	% of UCR	N	% of UCR
Murder/manslaughter	65	62	95.4	34	52.3
Robbery	1,554	324	20.8	120	7.7
Sex offenses (violent)	326	143	43.9	29	8.9
Assault	947	109	11.5	48	5.1
Total	2,892	638	22.1	231	8.0

[a]UCR denotes Uniform Crime Reports.

Table 6-4
Persons Indicted by Number of Prior Offenses

Number of Prior Offenses	Total[a]		Violent		Nonviolent	
	N	%	N	%	N	%
0	235	68.7	307	89.8	262	76.6
1	57	16.7	29	8.5	54	15.8
2	31	9.1	3	0.9	19	5.6
3	11	3.2	2	0.6	9	2.6
4	5	1.5	1	0.3	1	0.3
5	2	0.6	–	–	1	0.3
6	1	0.3	–	–	–	–
Totals	342	100.0	342	100.0	342	100.0

[a]The nonviolent and violent offender columns are not mutually exclusive. The total is not a sum of those columns.

sentence of five years net imprisonment. To restate Option I, if any member of the cohort had an adult felony conviction of any sort in the five-year period before 1973, then the charges and convictions recorded in that year would be considered to have been prevented.

Under Option I, we find that 68 offenders would have been prevented from committing an offense in 1973, which is 19.9 percent of the cohort. (See table 6-5.) These individuals were responsible for 115 counts of violent crime. But at the conviction level, only 54 counts of violence would have been prevented by the Option I sentencing policy. Note that these 68 persons committed 115 offenses which would not have been carried out if the Option I sentencing policy

Table 6-5
The Impact of Option Iᵃ on the Amount of Crime Prevented, Arrest Level, and Conviction Level

	Persons Indicted	Persons Prevented		1973 UCR Violent Crimes	Counts Prevented			
					Arrest Level		Conviction Level	
		N	% of Indicted		N	% of UCR	N	% of UCR
Murder/manslaughter	36	7	19.4	65	18	27.7	9	13.8
Robbery	128	36	28.1	1,554	64	4.1	30	1.9
Sex offenses (violent)	79	8	10.1	326	21	6.4	5	1.8
Assault	49	4	8.2	927	12	1.3	9	1.0
Multiple offenses (two of the above)	50	13	26.0	–	–	–	–	–
Totals	342	68	19.9	2,892	115	4.0	54	1.9

ᵃOption I: a five year net prison term imposed after any felony conviction; no violent felonies are required.

were applied; this modest total represents 4.0 percent of the 2892 crimes of violence reported during 1973. But there were only 54 of these 115 preventable counts that resulted in convictions, or 1.9 percent of the reported crimes.

Another comparison would be that of crimes prevented as a portion of crimes cleared. The 115 prevented counts of violence are 18.0 percent of the 638 violent crimes cleared by arrest. While three and one-half times higher than the 4.0 percent figure, it is still small in light of the severity of Option I.

These findings are well within the ranges suggested by the models proposed by Clarke and Greenberg. The Shinnars' estimate cannot be reconciled with our findings, especially since for adults Option I is more severe than any policy they suggest.

Option II also calls for a mandatory sentence of five years, but it focuses on recidivist offenders. It is the most severe sentence applicable only to recidivists among the options considered here. (See table 6-6.)

Under this option, 28 of the 342 indictees, charged with 43 violent offenses, would have been prevented from committing these offenses in 1973 if this sentencing policy had been in effect. The percentage of Franklin County violence would have been reduced by 1.5 percent.

The results of Option III-V are shown in table 6-7. It is apparent that none of these variants on the severe sentencing policy of Option I would have prevented as much as the 4.0 percent of violent crime which our most drastic sentencing policy would have averted. (Again, this 4.0 percent represents the proportion of 1973 violent crimes prevented by incapacitation of the total number of violent crimes reported in Franklin County.)

But if Option I were mandated by the statutes, every felon would serve a five-year sentence, even if the offense involved nothing more serious than bad checks, larceny, or auto theft. The absurd results to which such a policy would lead are hardly offset by the preventive effect described here. But any more specific option would be even less effective in the prevention of violent crime.

Conclusions

Based then, on this research, it would seem that the conclusions of Clarke and Greenberg are supported. This study strongly suggests that incapacitation makes only a small and modest impact on the violent crime rate. What is the degree of this impact? Clearly, any projection must be imprecise because the accuracy of official crime statistics is far less than perfect. Nonetheless, based on official data, it is reasonably certain that the impact of incapacitation is low. Our strongest incapacitation policy, the impractically harsh Option I (five years net imprisonment for any previous felony), prevented about 4.0 percent of the reported violent crimes in the county and 18.0 percent of the violent crimes cleared by arrest and resulting in an official charge.

Table 6-6
The Impact of Option II[a] on the Amount of Crime Prevented, Arrest Level, and Conviction Level

| | | Persons Prevented | | 1973 UCR, Violent Crime | Counts Prevented | | | |
| | Persons Indicted | | | | Arrest Level | | Conviction | |
		N	% of Indicted		N	% of UCR	N	% of UCR
Murder/manslaughter	36	0	–	65	2	3.1	1	1.5
Robbery	128	18	14.1	1,554	28	1.8	15	1.0
Sex offenses (violent)	79	4	5.1	326	7	2.2	1	0.3
Assault	49	2	4.1	947	6	0.6	3	0.3
Multiple offenses (two of the above)	50	4	8.0	–	–	–	–	–
Totals	342	28	8.2	2,892	43	1.5	20	0.7

[a]Option II: a five year net prison term imposed after any second felony conviction; no violent felonies are required.

Table 6-7
Summary of the Impact of Five Sentencing Options

Measure of Prevention Sentencing Option Number	Persons Prevented	% of Cohort[a]	Indictment Charges Prevented	% of UCR[b]	Conviction Counts Prevented	% of UCR[b]
I	68	19.9	115	4.0	54	1.9
II	28	8.2	43	1.5	20	0.7
III	12	3.5	21	0.7	11	0.4
IV	44	12.9	71	2.5	28	1.0
V	21	6.1	41	1.4	24	0.8

[a]The cohort consisted of 342 indictees.

[b]There was a total of 2,892 violent felonies in Franklin County in 1973.

Option I: One or more convictions, no prior violent felony, five-year mandatory sentence.

Option II: Two or more convictions, no prior violent felony, five-year mandatory sentence.

Option III: Three or more convictions, no prior violent felony, five-year mandatory sentence.

Option IV: One or more convictions, no prior violent felony, three-year mandatory sentence.

Option V: One or more convictions, one violent felony required, five-year mandatory sentence.

Why doesn't incapacitation prevent more crime? This analysis suggests three reasons. First, our study did not assume the incapacitation of juveniles. Since in 1973 about one-fourth the persons arrested for violent crimes were juveniles, (Table 30, 1973 *Uniform Crime Reports*), stiffer policies that leave the juvenile system unaffected can have no impact on the incidence of juvenile violence. Certainly incapacitation of juvenile felony offenders would have prevented some violent crimes. Incapacitation policies applied to juvenile offenders would require a drastic modification of juvenile court legislation and the disposition of juvenile offenders.

Second, at least according to this study, the pool of violent recidivists who would have been immobilized through incapacitation is comparatively small in comparison to all those indicted for violent offenses. *Over two-thirds of the persons in this study were first-time felony offenders. Incapacitation could not have prevented their 1973 crimes.* Only 31 percent of the cohort had any previous felony conviction. Only 11 percent of the cohort had any previous *violent* felony conviction. Fourteen percent of the cohort had two or more felonies of any type. The potential target groups are too small for incapacitation to be truly effective.

Third, the rate of repetition for the recidivist group is too low to provide significant reductions in the incidence of crime through an incapacitation policy. The average interval between violent incidents for a repeat offender was 5.6

years; the median was 3.6 years. Probably some of this delay was caused by imprisonment; some was caused by difficulties in apprehending an offender after his return to crime. The typical offender in this cohort committed officially recorded violent crimes infrequently. The clearest example is the case of the most frequent offender. This man had six prior felony offenses and was convicted in 1973 of a seventh. Yet it took him forty years to acquire such a record. Two persons had five convictions; one began his felony career in 1937, the other in 1945. The implication is that career violent offenders commit their recorded crimes slowly, if persistently.

This finding contrasts sharply with the assumption of the Shinnars and others that career violent offenders commit a disproportionate share of the uncleared and uncharged murders/manslaughters, robberies, rapes, and assaults. If this assumption is true, then a strict incapacitation policy would indeed prevent more crime than projected in this study. It should be stressed, however, that police practice tends to overcharge and overclear those arrested. There is no reliable way to balance the impact of the conflicting biases (the Shinnars' assumption and police practice). For this reason we have avoided specific assumptions about the "real" and "total" criminality of those arrested and charged. Instead, we have relied on official data of clearance by arrest and police charge, and actual indictments. Using these data, we found that 342 persons were arrested for violent crimes; they were charged with 638 offenses of the 2892 reported. Sixty-eight arrestees would have been prevented from committing 115 personal crimes under the provisions of Option I. Again, 115/2892 is roughly 4 percent of the reported offenses. Similarly, 115/638 is 18 percent of the charge counts which would have been prevented under Option I.

The implication of this analysis is clear. The characteristics of the criminal population and the limits of the criminal justice process minimize the potential of incapacitation. Our findings show that those arrested for violent crime are primarily first offenders. The repeaters are recidivating at a much slower rate than the Shinnars assume. We conclude from our data that incapacitation is a much less effective tool in the reduction of crime than Wilson and van den Haag believe.

Wilson's recommendations for an incapacitation policy as a means of crime control are based on the Shinnar extrapolations and on the Wolfgang cohort study. Superficially, Wilson's suggestion has face validity. If, indeed, as Wolfgang noted, a certain small population of repeaters commit a large number of crimes in a short period, then simply slowing them down with incapacitation-oriented sentences ought to cut the crime rate.

This suggestion fails, however, when tested on an adult population. It seems likely that no matter how lax the adult criminal justice system may be, convicted felons do not return to crime as quickly as the repetitive juveniles in the Wolfgang study.

The possibility exists that this cohort, a collection of people in one county in one year, is atypical. Perhaps, for cities other than Columbus, the typical criminal population consists of a larger proportion of repeat offenders. We encourage replication of this study to test that possibility.

For incapacitation to be effective, two conditions must exist. First, the apprehension rate must be greatly increased, unless it can be shown that a very large percentage of uncleared crimes are committed by those who are arrested. Second, a large percentage of crimes must be committed by repeat offenders, much higher than has been found in this study. This second condition depends on the assumption that convicted offenders spend very little time in prison. Advocates of an incapacitation policy assume that both of these conditions are largely true. This study suggests that they are not.

Note

1. The cohort consists of all violent felony cases completed in 1973. Not all the cases began in 1973. Half the individuals were first booked in 1973 (50.0 percent), most of the rest in 1972 (45.6 percent) and the remainder in 1971 or before (4.4 percent). For simplicity in the study, the population is called the 1973 cohort and treated as if all cases began in 1973. This determination does not influence the results of the study, since the hypothetical incapacitation sentence is imposed on each person's record individually.

References

Clarke, Stevens H. 1974. "Getting 'Em Out of Circulation: Does Incarceration of Juvenile Offenders Reduce Crime?" *Journal of Criminal Law and Criminology* 65 (December): 528-535.

Ehrlich, Isaac. 1973. "Participation in Illegitimate Activities: A Theoretical and Empirical Investigation." *Journal of Political Economy* 81 (May/June): 521-568.

Greenberg, David F. 1975. "The Incapacitative Effect of Imprisonment: Some Estimates." *Law and Society Review* 9 (Summer): 541-580.

Shinnar, Shlomo, and Reuel Shinnar. 1975. "The Effects of the Criminal Justice System on the Control of Crime: A Quantitative Approach." *Law and Society Review* 9 (Summer): 581-612.

United States Department of Justice. Federal Bureau of Investigation. 1972. *Crime in the United States, 1972: Uniform Crime Reports.* Washington, D.C.: Government Printing Office, Tables 5 and 76.

United States Department of Justice. Federal Bureau of Investigation. 1973. *Crime in the United States, 1973: Uniform Crime Reports.* Washington, D.C.: Government Printing Office, Tables 5, 30, and 75.

van den Haag, Ernest. 1975. *Punishing Criminals: Concerning a Very Old and Painful Question.* New York: Basic Books.

Wilson, James Q. 1975. *Thinking About Crime.* New York: Basic Books.

Wolfgang, Marvin, Robert M. Figlio, and Thorsten Sellin. 1972. *Delinquency in a Birth Cohort.* Chicago: University of Chicago Press.

The Survival of the Fearful

John P. Conrad

The Crumbling of the Prison Community

The charting of the prison community is one of the favorite occupations of criminology. The first reconnaissance was made by Donald Clemmer in a modest account of his observations in Illinois prisons.[1] It has acquired the status of a classic because it was the first—and still one of the best—of a long succession of studies exploring this artificial community and its variants. Clemmer contributed a homely neologism, "prisonization," to refer to the socializing processes by which guards and prisoners together create the community in which the guards work and the prisoners live.

These processes are as ugly as the word; they constitute the acculturation of all concerned to deprivation and humiliation. The guard adjusts the values he brings to the prison to meet the necessities of security and control. He must distrust everyone around him; he must encourage the snitch and the tale-bearer; he must allow the convict no privacy. Beyond these reversals of personal standards, he must accustom himself to verbal abuse and to a nagging anxiety about his personal safety.

The prisoner's adjustment is more precarious. He brings values to the prison that are generally similar to the guard's. He too must learn to distrust others; he must make sexual adaptations that he would have found intolerable in the free world; he must expect no privacy at all. He too must submit to verbal abuse without retaliation. Even more than the guard, he must resign himself to physical danger from which he can never fully protect himself.

In addition to these adaptations, the prisoner must also *seem* to obey two inconsistent sets of rules. Official regulations control his every movement; noncompliance is subject to punishment, often unpredictably severe. He must also *seem* to comply with the convict code, which prescribes his social relationships and limits the degree to which he can safely cooperate with the guards or associate with convicts who are in violation of the prisoners' ethics. Necessity may require him to violate both sets of rules, but self-preservation mandates the appearance of conformity. Due regard for correct appearances is essential to social acceptance and to survival.

Thus both guard and convict are prisonized. Those on both sides of this equilibrium must accommodate to daily confrontations, any of which might erupt into a dangerous physical conflict. Maintaining the minimum levels of order and services requires that the rules be compromised. Guards usually

119

overlook minor infractions. Prisoners do inform on each other, in spite of principles to the contrary, when security is threatened by a fellow prisoner's unacceptable aggressions. Guard captains expect both codes to be frequently violated. The officer who enforces the rules to the letter will be instructed to use his common sense and discretion. Every morning, the captain will find anonymous "kites" under his door advising him of threats and improprieties that some prisoner has considered to need action by custody. Keepers make what concessions they must to assure that the kept will cooperate in the maintenance of order. Convicts must find ways to meet the seemingly impossible requirements of two opposed norms. They must protect themselves from the system's rigors and from each other. It is not surprising that many fail to achieve full prisonization. When a violation of either code comes to light the fall from grace may be precipitous. Time in the "hole," repeated often enough, will result in a label in the captain's office that cannot easily be eradicated. Known violation of the convict code results in ostracism at the least, and usually a reputation that makes the unhappy wretch a target for physical attack. The convict's prisonization is never easy; the wonder is that so many succeed in achieving it.

Clemmer initiated the investigation of these complex adaptations to the community within the walls. Sykes carried it further,[2] proposing a model of solidary opposition between the two castes occupying this austere and uneasy community. Sykes thought that tacit understandings about behavior enabled guards and convicts to keep a truce. These understandings call for loose enforcement of the rules by the guards, in return for which the prisoners will discourage the violence of hotheads who hope to break free of control. By Sykes's account, the traditional prison is always under the threat of overt conflict and disorder. Imprudent policy changes can rally "regular" prisoners to the side of nonconformists who wish to strike out against their oppressors and break the working truce. Even-handed management, tolerant of necessary compromise, can maintain the peace because peace serves the interests of everyone in the prison community.

Other investigations in the United States and in Europe have further documented the culture of muted confrontation that has characterized the modern prison. Variants of this culture in foreign prisons, in prisons for women, and in prisons that are units of large systems have been studied by investigators interested in the model's applicability to the many categories of penal reality.[3] While all these varieties of the prison culture differ markedly in the psychological and social adjustments that must be made by guards and convicts alike, one constant, if obvious, finding is the opposition of controllers with those controlled. Following Sykes, it is assumed that there is a solidarity on both sides. Guards set standards for their behavior with convicts that are both formally and informally enforced. Prisoners maintain a reciprocal set of standards for proper relationships with their keepers.

The existence of these arrangements cannot be doubted, but they are superstructures erected over deep and irreconcilable fissures within each faction. Neither guards nor convicts have ever constituted groups with homogeneous interests or values. Some of these fissures obviously result from the nature of the situation. As to the staff, the interests of the warden and his deputies are not those of the teachers and physicians who provide specialized service to the prisoners. The interests of neither group coincide with those of the guards patrolling a cell block or scanning the yard from a tower.

These divisions have always existed within the prison staff, and social change has accentuated them. The uniformed custodial staff was once subject to a discipline almost as humiliating as that imposed on the convicts.[4] But guards are now moving toward unionization—uncertainly and against obstacles imposed by their nervous superiors. Competing unions vie for their suffrage, thereby increasing the divisions within a staff once seen as peculiarly monolithic; the administrator's opposition to the affiliation of the guard line to an outside union further strains its solidarity.

The civil rights revolution also has added new strains. Prisoners now have rights, along with channels by which violations of these rights can be brought to official attention for remedy. The officer who formerly could count on his superiors' support, even when in the wrong, now feels himself caught between prisoners watchful for any deviation from prescribed conduct and superiors who seem all too ready to punish him at the behest of civil liberties organizations or the prisoners themselves.

In this climate it is not surprising that the control of prisoners is not the firm system that older employees think they remember. Whatever it once was—and the recollection of a halcyon peace within the walls is surely erroneous—control of the prison population is in more uncertain hands than ever before. The change in the guards' culture has been paralleled by changes in the convict culture, which have increased the hazards to both guard and convict.

Analysts of the prison community have concentrated their attention on the groupings within the convict population. "Square johns," "hall-busters," and "right guys" are archetypes enshrined in the sociology of the prison, even if the terminology seems anachronistic to the guard and convict of the seventies. This typology, so beloved by criminologists, depended on the dominant theme of opposition between keeper and kept and the varying adaptations of the latter to the former. It was thought that whatever prisoners felt about each other, their interests converged on the need to mitigate the pains of imprisonment by presenting a united front to the staff. "Right guys" predominated in this model of the prison population; their interests called for a sort of order in which a prisoner could do his time comfortably without intimidation from either guards or irresponsible fellow prisoners. There were always prisoners who would not subscribe to this adaptation to adversity. The "right guys" had to somehow restrain predators, informers, and the mentally unstable. With the tacit cooperation of the guards this control was usually accomplished. Thus the opposition between the staff and the convicts was kept at a level of accommodation in which the self-interests of both sides created a reliable truce.

It would be foolish to say that guard and prisoner are not in as much opposition as ever or that self-interests do not still prevail to keep the peace. But the peace is more precarious than ever before, and the self-interests on which it depends are generated by fears for life and limb. Divisions among the prisoners have radically changed so that the familiar social organization discovered in the observations taken in the forties and fifties no longer describes the present situation. New interprisoner conflicts have been generated, and the traditional controls are plainly inadequate to resolve them.

In the traditional prison, conflict among prisoners had two principal sources: predation and distrust. Strong prisoners intimidated and exploited the weak, sometimes for sex, sometimes for improvised stimulants, sometimes for candy bars. Weak prisoners protected themselves by seeking the favor of guards, which could most easily be gained by providing information. Both predator and informer could usually be kept within bounds by the social organization of the prisoners and the powerful controls in the hands of the administration through the manipulation of the indeterminate sentence structure. The informer was never safe from his fellow prisoners, and the too obviously aggressive prisoner exposed himself to the risk of an extended sentence. The system was adequate for the maintenance of control against these kinds of challenge.

Predators and informers have not vanished from the prison scene. The stakes have risen and social change has radically revised the fabric of prison society. Instead of the benzedrine inhalers and glue for sniffing that constituted the contraband of the fifties and before, prisoners now enjoy the choice of amphetamines, barbiturates, and marijuana, with a considerable amount of heroin coming into some fortresses. Prisoners are far more affluent than they used to be, partly because many of them have connections with narcotics traffic outside. It has become worthwhile to organize the maintenance of a drug traffic within the walls and to protect it from custodial interference.

The creation of cohesive organizations was beyond the capacity of prisoners in the traditional penitentiary. Few had any experience of organizations in the free world, and the methods of intelligence gathering used by custody assured that the frail gangs that occasionally developed could be readily broken down. Wardens interested in maintaining control instinctively knew that they could not allow prisoners to organize.

That was the traditional prison. It was predominantly white; the black admixture in the population seldom rose above 10 percent, if that high. Black prisoners were usually docile, outnumbered as they were and accustomed as they were to an intimidated minority status in the community. The relationship between white guards and white prisoners might be stormy at times, but the kinds of accommodations that relaxed codes of conduct on both sides in the interest of order were relatively easy to make. Shared values made for understanding, even during the turbulent confrontations.

The demographic change in American prisons has reduced the feasibility of the traditional arrangements. From a typical representation of 10 percent in most prisons, the black percentage has risen to 40 percent in some, and up to 80 percent in exceptional situations. Chicano prisoners in western states number as many as 30 percent. The power of numbers is apparent to both ethnic groups, and the consequences have disturbed the old equilibrium. It is not too much to say that the change is from a prison in which force and intimidation by force were monopolized by custody to one in which the most intimidating force is now in the hands of prisoners. It is a community of fear. Fear of the guards can be allowed for, if the occasion of confrontation is avoided, the convict need not fear his keeper. But the potential for violence in the hands of other prisoners, especially those of other races or belonging to other gangs, is unpredictable. In many prisons the surest hope of survival for the unaffiliated prisoner is voluntary segregation in protective units. Increasing numbers of prisoners are choosing to survive by this means, even at the cost of serving their sentences in solitary confinement.

The precursor of organized minority group power in the penitentiary was the Black Muslim movement as it surfaced in the late fifties and early sixties. Where Muslims achieved organizations of significant size, custody officials were alarmed and instinctively acted to repress them, usually with little success. They recognized the threat posed by a cohesive group of prisoners that was relatively impenetrable because of race and a discipline derived from doctrine. It was not until much later that some prison administrators saw that there was much to be valued in an organization that required its members to abstain from sexual promiscuity, narcotics, gambling, and other activities that are to be officially discouraged.

Although the prison gangs that began to gain power in the middle sixties in California and Illinois certainly were not copies of the Muslim movement, the example of Muslim power was not lost on the gang leadership. The disciplined organization of minority group prisoners could serve purposes other than religious. Black prisoners, drawn from the least powerful and most oppressed element in the population of the country, could in the arena of the prison acquire formidable powers through the solidarity of the gang.

The cohesion of the black and Chicano gangs is reinforced by the status of race relations in the cities. The vast change in the nature and quality of these relations needs no review here. But as a consequence of these changes, the typical black and Chicano offender arrives in prison a far different person from his predecessor of twenty years ago.

The new black prison population is aggressive, resentful of the real and painful grievances of blacks everywhere, and often disposed to express accumulated anger in ways that intimidate or harm white inmates. Differences among black prisoners evaporate when they are in confrontation with whites—guards or fellow prisoners. Solidarity among white inmates is seldom achieved, even in such confrontations, despite the occasional coalescence of such gangs as the

Neo-Nazis or the Aryan Brotherhood. It cannot be far from the truth to assert that the single most significant change in the prison community during the past decade is the pre-eminence of race conflict among the problems of control in the prison community. Whether organized or not, this conflict has permanently modified the old equilibrium and heightened tensions to the point that personal safety is the daily concern of both staff and prisoners in the megaprisons of the large states.

No one should be surprised, however. Americans have not yet succeeded in reconciling the races in the free community. For the black prisoner, aggression against white prisoners expresses a fury against white privilege that he has swallowed in silence when free. It also expresses a sense of power over whites that is denied him outside, but that becomes easily used in this community where he is a member of a majority.

The white inmate, now a minority—and a fragmented minority at that—is at a disadvantage for which outside experience has not prepared him. No longer does he have access to the support of a majority or the reliable support of the apparatus of power. He is the target of abuse and sexual molestation against which he cannot safely retaliate. In some prisons white gangs may provide some protection, but the Neo-Nazis and the Aryan Brotherhood will not welcome him unless he is an effectual combatant or, sometimes, willing to trade sexual favors for someone's strong right arm.

Prison gangs seem to begin with attempts to create racial solidarity in the face of penal adversity. The solidarity is fragmented by an often murderous rivalry between gangs of the same ethnic group. In Illinois prisons, the Black P. Stone Nation, the Black Gangster Disciple Nation, and the Conservative Vice Lords, all ethnically black, manage an uneasy truce, and together they present the authorities with control problems that have not yet been contained successfully.[5] In California prisons, once citadels of custodial professionalism, such organizations as the Mexican Mafia, Nuestra Familia, the Black Guerilla Family, and the Aryan Brotherhood have forced the authorities to make unwelcome accommodations by dint of violence, both actual and threatened. Prison systems in other states with large metropolitan populations are confronted with similar gang configurations, impressively cohesive and skillful in leadership. Gang discipline is strict and based on each member's complete commitment to the organization.

Each gang has derived strength from lines of communication and support to membership on the streets. There is an interesting difference, in this respect, between the Illinois prison gang and its counterpart in California. The Illinois "supergangs" are, in effect, prison chapters of large and powerful Chicago gangs, mostly composed of young unemployed blacks. Transposed to the prison, these gangs develop into adult groups with membership far more advanced in years than their active fellow members on the streets.

In California, the two most powerful gangs seem to be Chicano, and both originated in prisons. The Mexican Mafia was organized in 1957 as an informal organization of Chicano inmates at the Deuel Vocational Institution at Tracy, then an institution intended for the confinement of the older wards of the California Youth Authority and the youngest prisoners of the Department of Corrections. Its functions were the collection of debts, gambling operations, and the distribution of narcotics. Most of its members hailed from East Los Angeles. As time has gone on, the Mexican Mafia has taken in members from other large cities. Its organizational cohesion has increased over the two decades of its history, and through ruthless action against its rivals and nonaffiliated prisoners it has achieved a position of unprecedented power in such prisons as San Quentin and Folsom.

Nuestra Familia began as a protective society for prisoners ineligible for the Mexican Mafia because of their nonmetropolitan origins. Using much the same organizational methods, Nuestra Familia has achieved power comparable to the Mexican Mafia's at the Deuel Vocational Institution. Hostilities between the two gangs have reached such an intensity that members of one cannot be housed safely in a prison "controlled" by members of the other. On this issue, the California authorities have tacitly conceded that it is futile to contest its legal authority against the realities as defined by gang hostilities. Transfer policy between institutions has taken due notice of the murderous relations between the two gangs, and the incidence of murder has accordingly declined. There is, however, some indication that the murders that the prison system can prevent by physical separation are merely deferred until release. The gangs that began in the prison continue their warfare on the streets—a paradoxical reversal of the gang hostilities in Illinois.

The measure of the power of these gangs is to be found in the prison segregation units. Fear of their power and of their members' willingness to murder at the command of their leaders has driven unprecedented numbers of convicts into the haven of protective custody. Many of these fugitives from the "hit men" of the prison yard have been aggressors themselves; realists, they have known when they were outnumbered and have scurried to shelters that they ordinarily would have scorned. At the other end of the security block are the gang leaders, identified and immured by custody, but still in control of their followers through devious communication systems set up with prisoner cleaning crews, visiting wives and relatives, and occasional complaisant guards.

There continues to be the flow of rule violators into and out of the security block. Some will stay briefly in retribution for a minor infraction that could not be overlooked. Others will serve one long stretch—two weeks to a month—and return to the yard sufficiently chastened to mend their ways. A few, because of gang activities, may serve long periods of confinement because to the prison staff there seems to be no other effective alternative.

In most prisons the regime is more lenient than it used to be. Television, intercell chess games, and a supply of paperback novels divert the prisoner in his solitude, whereas his predecessors in former years had only the Bible for solace. The days are relatively quiet; many prisoners sleep off the nightly pandemonium to which most segregation units seem to be inclined. Isolated prisoners still throw excrement at their keepers, burn mattresses, and stop their plumbing to flood the cell block. Perhaps because of these retaliations for real or fancied grievances, perhaps because of the civil rights pressures on prison administration, perhaps because of the changed temper of the times, the old rigors of isolation are less common. Diet restrictions, requirements to stand at the bars during the daylight hours, and the threat of transfer to a dark strip cell are all becoming uncommon. It is still a place of coercion and misery, but the accommodations made by custody reflect the awareness that the imposition of meaningless rigors merely adds difficulties to the guard's task.

A convict in a Washington prison, in the "hole" for eighteen months, and more articulate than most who undergo this experience, described it like this:

Once the barred door to your cell slams shut, you're on your own as far as developing something to occupy your time. Nothing is available to you in the way of programming—you have no means at your disposal—it's just you, a few sheets of paper, a pencil or a pen, maybe a paperback novel or two, and the bare walls. Meal times are no joy. The food is dished up on trays by the R-1 kitchen crew so you intentionally receive small portions because that leaves more food for the kitchen crew and the officers. R-1 residents bring the tray to your cell and slide it under the door—so sometimes part of your food is scraped off under the door, and hair or dirt is often present in the food after this unsanitary delivery process. Any relief from the tedium of deadlock comes at shower time and yard time. Once a day, for ten minutes, you are allowed out to take a shower. Every day for one hour you're let out into a covered, fenced in cage—semi-outdoors. The only recreational equipment . . . is yourself and the walls.

The "hole" defines the prevailing limit of unacceptable behavior by the nature and misconduct of those confined in it. In prisons less troubled by gang and race problems, prisoners found in the "hole" are guilty of attempts to escape, possession of contraband, abusive language to officers, or refusal to work. In the huge prison systems of the larger states, some prisoners are confined on such charges as these, but a much larger concern is the concentration of exceptionally violent prisoners.

For example, in March 1977, the security housing units (to use their current designation) of the California prisons contained a total of 540 prisoners. A distribution by offense for that month is not available, but a previous study for December 1976 showed that more than half had been locked up for offenses involving extreme violence, including over forty prison homicides. The security housing units have had about the same capacity for the last ten years, but they are now full almost continuously. In addition to those segregated for the protection of the institution, there were in the same month 344 men housed in protective custody units, an unprecedentedly high number that has risen from about a tenth that number twenty years ago. Thus 1088 prisoners have been immobilized by their own violence or by the fear of it. That was about 6 percent of the total California prison population of 18,188 on the day of the survey.[6]

The number of prisoners in protective and administrative segregation is a rough measure of the impact of fear on the prison climate. But violence has had other impacts that are not to be gauged statistically. No numbers will measure the change wrought in prisoner-guard relations described in this statement by a senior member of the headquarters staff of the California department:

Social contacts between officers and inmates are getting more distant. When I was on the line, I would get assignments like supervision of a dormitory on the third watch (4 p.m. to midnight) and sometimes I got pretty scared. I'd be alone, and my chief protection was that I knew guys and they knew me and we had a sort of rapport. I was always talking with them. But now, on account of the violence, we've had to introduce a sort of buddy system, and I won't say we could have avoided it. The officers do their patrolling in pairs. They rap with each other and hardly ever talk with the inmates. They don't need to. In the days when an officer was alone on a cell block or in a dorm, he wouldn't have anybody to talk to except the inmates he was working with. I'm convinced that that kind of interaction was helpful and important, but we're losing it. We don't know what's going on, and we don't have an opportunity or occasion to build rapport.

This is a community of the fearful in which identities have been reduced to guard, aggressor, and victim, a triangle of latent violence that is destructive of the attributes from which human interaction becomes possible. At best, the prison's effectiveness in achieving the resocialization of offenders has been marginal and probably the result of intimidation rather than any positive and directed effort. Obviously, many contemporary prisoners will be thoroughly intimidated by their sojourn in these fortresses of violence. For those who have lived through the terror, either by inflicting it or by fleeing from it into custodial protection, the damage must be severe and the prospects for future community adjustment, gravely impaired.

Desocialization Within the Walls

The Dangerous Offender Project has from the first been concerned with the rising level of violence in U.S. prisons. We have considered it probable that the balance of terror in the megaprison reflects the violence of the community from which prisoners come and to which they return. They brought violence into the prison; they take it out.

We have undertaken a study of violence as reflected by the numbers and nature of the convicts segregated from prison general populations. Inventories have been taken of these categories of prisoners in six different and widely separated states. This chapter draws on a completed fragment of our study at the

Washington State Penitentiary at Walla Walla, one of the most remote fortresses of American prisons. Situated in the extreme southwest of the state, it is at a maximum possible distance from Washington's major population centers on the Puget Sound. Built in the last quarter of the nineteenth century, it has a "rated capacity" of 1420 prisoners. In recent years the actual population has oscillated from a peak of 1604 in September 1966 to a low of 902 in April 1974 and to another high, in June 1977, of nearly 1700. Until April 1975, its maximum security unit was a cell block with a capacity of 100, distributed among four tiers. The top tier was a unit of twenty-four cells, set aside for prisoners requiring protection from enemies in the general population. The remaining three tiers were distributed among three classes of problem prisoners. Those assigned to "Administrative Segregation" were men who, after a hearing, were determined to be a threat to the security of the institution or to someone, either staff or prisoner, in the institution, or occasionally, in danger *from* someone, according to information in the hands of the administration. No specific infraction would occasion this classification; the opinion of the staff determined it. A second class consisted of men assigned to "Segregation," who had been found guilty of some institutional infraction. Their terms were relatively brief and they were allowed some privileges such as exercise, books from the library, and other amenities. The third class, "Isolation," was reserved for those found guilty of the most serious infractions, usually involving overt violence.

In April 1975 the maximum security cell block was found inadequate to contain all its commitments. A tier was found in an adjacent unit for the protective custody class, thereby freeing space for the refractory prisoners who were being locked up in greater numbers. At the same time, it was found that increasing numbers of men were seeking protection. A second tier was soon allocated for this purpose. In January 1976, the protection unit was moved to a wing of its own, consisting of 128 cells. What was happening was an impressive explosion of the numbers of prisoners requiring rigorous control. Some idea of the changed dimensions of the population can be gained from table 7-1.

This steep rise in the maximum security population is primarily attributable to prisoners asking for protection. Of the 197 sequestered in September 1976, 117 claimed that they were in danger in the general population. Six months earlier, there were 98 out of a total of 167. These high figures contrast with varying numbers in former years, always well within the capacity of the twenty-four-cell tier that was assigned for protective custody. In the early sixties, the number requiring protection was as low as 4.

The Walla Walla experience could be duplicated in almost every maximum security prison; it is worse in states like California or Illinois. There is some chance that the overcrowding of prisons may be reduced as the crime rate declines because of an aging population, although this popular prediction is by no means a certainty. Such a respite is unlikely to extend to the segregated population. Prisons have become repositories for the containment of violent

Table 7-1

September Population of Washington State Penitentiary, 1966-1976, Showing Total Population and Numbers Assigned to Maximum Security Units

Year	Total Population	Maximum Security Population	Percent in Maximum Security
1966	1604	60	3.7
1967	1345	36	2.7
1968	1232	39	3.2
1969	1184	60	5.1
1970	1305	52	4.0
1971	1151	27	2.3
1972	1012	26	2.6
1973	981	34	3.5
1974	1076	51	4.6
1975	1327	112	8.4
1976	1588	197	12.4

criminals. The pressures of economics and reform have coincided to diminish the leaven of nonviolent offenders. The emphasis on violence has increased the expectation of it both among staff and among prisoners.

For some, the reputation for extreme violence is protection in itself. For others, enmeshed in the special culture of the prison gang, such a reputation will enhance prestige among peers. In the classic prison culture described by the writers of the fifties, the "gorilla" was a loner, feared by other prisoners but usually ostracized as a person with mental problems. His internment in the "hole" was considered an appropriate decision by custody.

At Walla Walla and prisons like it in medium sized or small states the archetypical "gorilla" can still be found. One such prisoner, seething in solitary anger for over six years, told us that he wanted no more than thirty minutes on the yard, which he would use to kill an old enemy. He would then be content to spend the rest of his life in his cell in the security block. Vengeance and fear had converted a man into no more than a combination of killer and victim.

The process seldom goes so far, but it works on all who are stowed in these barren tiers. A preliminary assessment of the criminal careers of men released from Walla Walla after prolonged sojourn in segregation indicates that over three-quarters of them are back in prison within a year. Such a result is hardly surprising; the desocialization of the "hole" inflicts damage for which there can be no adequate remedy.

For the exceptionally violent convict in the prisons drawing from large metropolitan ghettoes and barrios, the situation is different but even more serious. Accounted a "heavy" and confirmed as such by his segregation, he still goes through the same kind of experience as the "gorilla" and is subject to the same rage about it. His commitment to his gang will not allow him to desist from the violence that required his segregation. Very probably he will take the same commitment to aggression back to the streets.

The necessity for restraint can hardly be disputed. It is time that alternate controls should be conceived and tested. The continuing study under way by the Dangerous Offender Project is only one of the possible avenues to change. In a less murderous climate, innovation might flourish because of the urgency. It is understandable that administrators hesitate to modify the barbarous arrangements that they must impose on these tragic young people, and our inquiries have uncovered none who have taken this risk. Our investigation of the characteristics and experiences of these populations is conducted in the expectation that increased understanding will facilitate desperately needed experimentation.

Reconnaissance of segregation practices throughout the country uncovers neither experimentation nor innovation. The need for the protection of vulnerable prisoners in Illinois is so great that the old prison at Joliet has been virtually converted into a protective custody facility. In Minnesota, a serious effort is under way to provide program and activity for prisoners in protective custody; a similar effort is under way in Washington State. But in a survey conducted in 1976 by our project, wardens of seventy maximum security prisons had no solutions to offer beyond the establishment of specialized institutions for the truly dangerous prisoner and the removal of the mentally disturbed from the penal process.[7]

Where the answers are so few, the questions must be numerous. Research under way by the Dangerous Offender Project will clarify a few of the issues by creating profiles of the kinds of prisoners who find their ways into solitary confinement and reporting the aftermath of their experience. The information thus assembled will constitute a foundation for hypotheses for experimentation.

Meanwhile, the questions abound. Most of them have been in the penal discourse for a long time, but none are close to resolution. To put them all in one place is a modest service, leading, we hope, to initiatives not now in sight. As we see them, these are the most urgent issues:

1. What kinds of behavior are considered by correctional administrators to require the isolation of a prisoner?
2. To what extent can the social influences determining these kinds of behavior be neutralized by administrative action?
3. To what extent can clinical or administrative intervention remedy psychological conditions productive of these kinds of behavior?
4. What kinds of daily routine can be instituted as standard for the control and health of the isolated prisoner?

5. What kinds of treatment and activity should be provided for the isolated prisoner?
6. Can systems of incentives be installed to program changes in the behavior of the isolated prisoner without unacceptable interference with his volition?
7. What signs of change should be accepted as evidence of readiness to return to the general prison population?
8. What programs should be standardized for post-isolation control and resocialization after the prisoner's return to the general population?
9. What are the psychological and social consequences of protracted terms served in isolation?
10. What constitutional and legal requirements of due process can be formulated to guide decision-making as to assignment to and release from isolation?
11. What is the statistical experience relative to isolation? To what extent and in what categories has the number of isolated prisoners increased?

The dilemma is cruel, and its cost in lives and values is increasingly severe. On the one side is the mounting prevalence of fear in the maximum security prison. Fear depersonalizes human relations; enemies are identified by group or status, not by actions or human attributes. Self-protection becomes an obsession, driving from the mind concerns about self-improvement and plans for a better future. For staff, the anxiety about personal safety inevitably modifies benign attitudes towards prisoners into stereotyped hostility. Clearly, the dangerous prisoner cannot be allowed to have the freedom of the prison yard, thereby confirming in his fellow prisoners' minds the belief that their keepers are indifferent to their safety and incompetent to maintain order and security.

That necessary policy forces the prison manager to the other horn of the dilemma. To create a prison within a prison in which people are caged like animals, to keep them there without program or incentives to change is to concede that the only ultimate control is intimidation, for the experience of isolation has no other meaning. The prisoner is contained in the most adverse conditions consistent with the conscience of his keepers. The only positive expectation the staff can entertain is that the experience will be so wretched that it will induce the convict to submit to the rules rather than to risk repeating the experience. Undeniably, this process works with many, but the costs have yet to be reckoned. For those for whom the experience of solitary confinement holds no further terrors, the reckoning adds up to everyone's complete defeat.

It is not in the nature of a prison or a system of prisons to succeed. Failures populate these fortresses and justify them. There are degrees of failure, however, and it is the business of the prison official to minimize avoidable misery and loss. The prevalence of fear in American prisons has accentuated their failure. In some prisons anarchy is in sight, and irresolute administrators contribute to the decay of the control of violence. Confidence can be restored only by managers who know what they are doing and why. It is tragic that social science has so little guidance to offer them when they need it most.

Notes

1. Donald Clemmer, *The Prison Community* (New York, Rinehart and Company, 1958), pp. 300-302.

2. Gresham Sykes, *The Society of Captives* (Princeton, N.J.: Princeton University Press, 1958).

3. See Thomas Mathiesen, *The Defenses of the Weak* (London: Tavistock Publications, 1965) for an account of the social relationships in a Norwegian prison. See Terence Morris and Pauline Morris, *Pentonville, A Sociological Study of an English Prison* (London: Routledge and Kegan Paul, 1963), for a view of the English prison community differing to a considerable extent from Sykes' findings. Rose Gialombardo, *Society of Women: A Study of a Women's Prison* (New York: Wiley, 1966) was the first and still is one of the most comprehensive accounts of the incarcerative model as applied to the female offender. David A. Ward and Gene G. Kassebaum, *Women's Prison: Sex and Social Structure* (Chicago: Aldine, 1965) presents an alternate theoretical approach. For a more recent account of the women's prison, see Esther Heffernan, *Making It In Prison: The Square, the Cool and the Life.* (New York: Wiley-Interscience, 1972). For a view of the prison as a unit in a large system, see the study of the California Men's Colony by Gene G. Kassebaum, David A. Ward, and Daniel M. Wilner: *Prison Treatment and Parole Survival* (New York: Wiley, 1971).

4. This topic has seldom been so candidly explored as in James B. Jacobs' recent *Stateville: The Penitentiary in Mass Society* (Chicago: University of Chicago Press, 1977), pp. 39-41. The career of the guard in the prison of the nineteenth century and the first half of the twentieth century is a topic that will soon slip out of the access of social historians as the last veterans of that era become unavailable to tell the story of their position as the oppressed oppressors.

5. Jacobs, pp. 138-174.

6. Data supplied by the Management Information Service of the California Department of Corrections.

7. Robert A. Freeman, Simon Dinitz, and John P. Conrad, "The Bottom Is in the Hole," *American Journal of Corrections* 39, no. 1 (January-February 1977): 25-31.

8

Right, Wrong, and Sheer Indifference: Ethics for the Correctional Pragmatist

John P. Conrad

Technology and Ethics: A Collision Course?

One fine morning not so many years ago, when I was chief of research of the United States Bureau of Prisons, I was summoned to the Director's office for a staff discussion of Bureau policy related to the use of inmates as test subjects for addictive drugs. Our director, Myrl Alexander, liked to bring in the staff for help in the resolution of any issue where the indicated decision was not apparent. That was the situation on the morning of this special meeting.

The question over which we were to agonize that morning originated with a request from the Public Health Service for assistance in testing new analgesics for their addictive properties and correct dosage. For many years this function had been carried out at Public Health Service hospitals by using as subjects confirmed heroin addicts who were patients in those facilities. Unfortunately, changes in law and policy had eliminated the supply of untreatable addicts in the service's care. There was reason to believe that the bureau had in its custody an ample number for its testing program. Could we arrange to concentrate a few of them at a convenient prison so that the testing program could proceed? As I recall, no inducements were to be held out to the prisoners accepting assignment to this program other than administration of the drugs themselves; there was no question of pay or early parole consideration.

It was an accurate assumption that we had suitable subjects for the project. There was no doubt that the terms of the project would be attractive to those qualified and to many who were not. This was not a decision-making meeting in which statistical data were to be required of me so that the logistics of the undertaking could be planned. The question was a matter of ethics, and the discussion was carried on in that unfamiliar vocabulary.

Everyone was uncomfortable about the request and its implications. The ethical chasm is easy to chart. On the one hand there was a practical utilitarianism. The needs of the Public Health Service were stated in terms of the greatest good for the greatest number. The medical profession had to calibrate the addictive properties of new drugs so that treatment could be administered with the benefits intended, and without unanticipated side effects. Obviously, human subjects were needed to carry out the tests. The risks would be acceptable to the subjects to be selected; none of them would be likely to object to the probability of again becoming addicted to a narcotic. The benefits of the

133

project would accrue to thousands, perhaps millions, of patients. All that would be necessary to achieve these benefits was access to a small group of peculiar people who had been so heavily addicted in the past that there could be no doubt of their future return to drugs. They would volunteer; there was no question of coercion or disregard of the requirements of informed consent. No one would be selected for the program who did not meet minimum criteria of age, length of addiction, and failure to benefit from previous treatment programs.

So what was the problem? What made us so uneasy? Against the utilitarianism of the medical officers of the Public Health Service there was the conditioning of a correctional staff. We sincerely, if muddleheadedly, believed that our job was to design and carry out programs that would restore prisoners to society as functioning citizens. To engage in experimentation and the testing of opiates, even for such obviously desirable objectives, was to give up on the people we were supposed to help. Even though the subjects were willing—and we had no illusions that they were not—to administer these drugs to them was to do them harm. To make the exception requested of us was to run counter to the bureau's whole philosophy. We had to assume that each of our prisoners was reclaimable if we could find the right treatment program for him. That would include the confirmed addict, regardless of the duration of his reliance on narcotics.

Of course, we had not come close to discovering an effective intervention for such people. That led to the resolution of our agonies, and we made a pained decision to comply with the request of the Public Health Service. In the course of that long morning, the director expressed his regret that we did not have a staff expert on ethics who could advise him on the findings of his discipline just as I would advise him about the advances of criminological research or the chief budget analyst would tell him about his fiscal choices.

The profundity of our discussion does not make this incident memorable, but its unique character does. Out of my long career as a correctional staff official, it is the only occasion I can remember when extended discourse on an ethical problem took place. Outside the correctional establishment, reputations are made and lost in controversies about what is morally permissible in the punishment of criminals. Since my emergence from the bureaucracy I have engaged in some of these controversies myself. Some critics imply that the lack of attention to ethical issues by correctional leaders is evidence of sheer indifference to them. We do well to be suspicious of the principles of the bureaucratic pragmatist, but I think something can be said in defense of the placidity of the directors and commissioners in the face of ethical dilemmas. In the nineteenth century, eminent moralists gave a great deal of attention to these matters and created principles for the governance of prisons that permeate our rhetoric and our thought, if not always our official conduct. We need only call to mind the pronouncements of such men as Bentham, Shaftesbury, and Mill in

England, and of the remarkable group that constituted the American Prison Congress of 1870 and issued its famous Declaration of Principles. When reformers have called the leaders of penology to account, it is to these standards that these leaders have been held. There may be considerable exasperation with the legal requirements of due process, but no responsible correctional administrator disputes the place of due process in prisons. To do so would be to deny the fundamentals of justice. They would lose legitimacy to their claim to be a part of a system of justice.

Faced with the familiar problems of crime and the administration of justice, our usual difficulty has been to choose the least bad of an array of possible decisions. We have generally known what we should do even though we have not always done it. The doctrines inherited from the nineteenth century, buttressed by precedent and experience, have provided inconspicuous but consistent ethical guidance.

What confronts us today is a set of new questions to which the comfortably vague ethics of the past cannot be applied easily. Technology prods us onto unfamiliar ground. New choices in the control of offenders confront us as a result of biomedical and psychological research. We have to review all over again the balance between the utilitarian goal of the greatest good for the greatest number and our own conditioning to do no needless harm and, if possible, to do some good.

A reminiscence from the fairly recent past will illustrate my point. In 1974, Kenneth Schoen, the commissioner of corrections of the state of Minnesota, organized a "Delphi" exercise to determine the probable future requirements of corrections in his state. An imposing group of experts was queried about reasonable expectations of the future incidence of crime, the need for prison space, and the probable nature of the offenders with whom the public would be most concerned. There was general agreement that for a long time it would be necessary to provide custodial control for dangerous offenders to ensure their incapacitation. There was some difference of opinion about the probable numbers of such prisoners and for how long their confinement would be necessary, but there was a reluctant but general consensus on the basic need. At one point in the discussion, however, an eminent psychiatrist in the Delphi panel commented that the discourse had an element of unreality to him. In 1974 there was no choice but to lock up the dangerous offender. Ten or twenty years hence, biomedical technology would give us a choice. Psychopharmaceutical drugs, psychosurgery, and the sophisticated use of behavior modification promised controls that would drastically reduce the need for incarceration, even for the dangerous offender. Disturbing and difficult ethical considerations would have to be settled. But we would have to face them. Could society continue to accept the justifications of incarceration that have prevailed with so little question for the last two centuries when control could be achieved without resort to so ugly and unnatural an institution as imprisonment?

What was presented for our consideration had to do with a future that is still conjectural despite some sanguine predictions from optimists eager to change not only the world but all the wicked people in it. The psychiatric expert on that Delphi panel is not the only person who has heard these strange messages from the laboratories. Research now under way does indeed point to major changes ahead in the human condition, and many of these changes will have their first impact on offenders facing sentences from the court. Chapter 4 in this book details the apparent possibilities; my concern here is to explore the ethical implications of potential biomedical interventions if and when they become practical alternatives to incarceration. I do not foresee a need for a new ethical doctrine to govern our choice of alternatives, but we may have to engage in unfamiliar efforts to achieve an acceptable justification for our decisions.

Scientism in the Hole

Let me begin with one of the easier problems ahead. The psychiatrist on the Delphi panel mentioned behavior modification as an alternative to incarcerative methods. Great things may still be expected from imaginative social scientists working with behavior modification concepts,[1] but I doubt that we will ever have behavior modification techniques powerful enough for us to dispense with the secure cell block for the genuinely dangerous offender. But consider a more moderate and plausible initiative.

Some years ago, the Bureau of Prisons had a furor on its hands because of a young psychologist at its Medical Center in Springfield, Missouri, who had developed a scheme to program inmates out of administrative segregation through a schedule of reinforcements. The project was called by the uncommunicative title, Special Treatment and Rehabilitative Training program so as to facilitate the working acronym, Project START. A fairly full account of the program can be found in a report of the General Accounting Office,[2] but the features necessary for this discussion can be easily outlined.

An inmate would be designated for the program because he was disruptive, dangerous to staff and others, predatory on weaker inmates, or disobedient to prison rules and regulations. He could be referred from any of the bureau's facilities, but admission was a decision reserved for the director of the bureau. Inmates accepted for Project START were programmed through nine stages of lessening austerity in living conditions. A week of compliance with requirements at each level of the program entitled the inmate to advance to the next level. Eventually, the prisoner would be entitled to return to the general population where, it was assumed, he would naturally want to be. The project was not well designed or well equipped—the facilities used were so inappropriate as to defeat the purposes of the program from the beginning—but that is not the point for this discussion.

What was remarkable was the outcry by prison reformers, social scientists, moral philosophers, and radical critics of criminal justice. It was angrily asserted that Project START was oppressive tinkering with the personal integrity and civil rights of the unfortunate men who were subjected to it. The Bureau of Prisons has never relished controversy, and it soon found that the cost of the project was too great to continue it. It was no great loss to penology but certainly an eloquent testimonial to the power of uninformed rhetoric.

In all that public discussion, nobody considered the nature of the alternative to START, the noisome "hole" that exists in every prison system. Prison segregation is a hideous affair. Men are confined in the hole because prison officials don't know what else to do with them. The principle is that segregation is maintained to protect prisoners in the general population from the violence of a small minority who can be controlled in no other way. Obviously, this principle can be violated by the capricious, prejudiced, or incompetent prison official. Nevertheless, some prisoners are indeed so dangerous to others that they have to be set apart. They do not rot there, as is so often claimed, but they survive, sometimes for many years. Their monotonous life is enlivened by vicious little conspiracies and occasional eruptions of physical violence against guards or each other. It is a wretched existence for all concerned.

Why was Project START thought to be so unacceptable an alternative? It was an experiment, the volition of the participants was not engaged, and the objectives were to change attitudes and behavior without that volition. Out of such materials a powerful emotional case can be made. The lessons to be drawn from the program's enforced termination are simple but worth our attention. In considering any alternative to an existing prison procedure, the reasons why it should be considered an improvement should be carefully defined. The most acceptable—indeed, the most essential reason—should be that the alternative provides a benefit to the prisoner that is not present in the existing procedure. It should also follow that no one will be intentionally harmed by the procedure and that unintended harm will be remedied. These obvious rules apply to any alternative. In the case of a program involving behavior modification, in which category there will be many more experiments, we should also specify three additional principles: prisoners should know what the experiment is about and what is expected of them; all agreements should be kept by the administration; and if the data do not clearly indicate the effectiveness of the program, appropriate modifications should be made or the program should be terminated. One of the inescapable realities of any bureaucracy—especially the prison is the temptation to rationalize persistence in a program long after it has been shown that it does not meet its stated objectives.

It is difficult to find an ethical basis for condemning behavior modification approaches that depend on positive reinforcement only. Negative reinforcements are part of everyone's life experience, and certainly they cannot be eliminated from prison life. Denial of a parole date, confinement in an isolation cell, or other penalties for a rule infraction are inescapable threats. They may be regarded as analogues of the negative reinforcements of everyday living. These relatively natural consequences of behavior differ from the artificial negative treatments, such as the administration of aversive conditioning by electric shock or even more radical interventions involving the administration of pain. Experiments of this kind in the coercive environment of the prison are impossible to justify when it is borne in mind that the purest intentions to help will be adulterated in their execution by casual decisions based on inadequate and misunderstood information. The lack of evidence that these techniques are successful when administered to persons outside the prison strengthens the position that they should not be administered to prisoners, even where consent has been obtained.

Ethical Limits for Chemical and Surgical Constraint

Much more explosive questions confront us in the prediction that chemical and surgical interventions may relieve us of the necessity to incarcerate someone because he is dangerous. Some conceptual underbrush should be cleared away before we proceed with the formulation of principles. First, there is every reason to believe that most violent offenses are committed by people who are unaffected by any organic pathology. To administer drugs to them or to attempt some kind of surgical intervention, with or without their consent, is a grotesque perversion of medicine. This is a violent society and the least significant cause of that violence is physiological. To pretend that there will ever be a medical magic bullet that will cause the ghetto mugger to put his gun and knife aside is the most contemptible kind of scientism.

Second, reports of such radical interventions as lobotomy, castration, and mysterious drugs have diverted us from more subtle and less well-understood interventions. The use of various tranquillizers and amphetamines is well established in many prisons and mental hospitals for the purposes of institutional order and security rather than for any long-range benefit to the individual. On that score many observers are quick to condemn the practice *a priori*. But before judgment is made, social scientists, at least, should be interested in getting the facts. Who gets these drugs and what is the outcome of their administration? What long-range harm is done? We do not hear much discussion of this problem, and what little we do hear is confounded by reference to the entirely different issue presented by the drugs which are said to have irreversible side effects that turn the unfortunate subject into a virtual vegetable. We can readily condemn that sort of treatment by referring to any accepted body of ethical precepts, but what about the drugs that merely make the recipient feel good or at least less hostile? Can we justify them on the grounds that they reduce the pains of incarceration for those who are subject to it? This is the kind of issue on which serious and ethically oriented people may differ. Until the facts on existing practice are collected, I must hold that the most significant pains of incarceration in this country result from the distresses inflicted on the prisoner by the American megaprison. To relieve these pains by drugs is to take the focus off the imperative to break up the fortress-prison and to create facilities on a human scale. I also know that hewing to an abstract principle like that will cause a good deal of avoidable suffering in the interest of a social goal of distant attainment. To help us to a better position, we need more facts.

A second question confronts us in the administration of drugs with specific but reversible effects on behavior. The example most often cited is progesterone, which reduces libido as long as dosage is regularly maintained but whose effects subside when treatment stops. Such a drug would have obvious value for the persistent sex offender and might be considered an acceptable substitute for castration. What is the ethical position if we present the confirmed sex offender with a choice: incarceration or an agreement to take the drug for as long as it is prescribed? This is not an entirely obvious problem to solve. First, it depends on our ability to make the prediction that recidivism is inevitable for some kinds of sex offenders. This prediction cannot be made more reliable than chance; the truth seems to be that, on the whole, most sex offenders do not recidivate and that some are successfully responsive to psychotherapy. Second, it offers the decision-maker an easy solution to a difficult problem. The fact that this drug succeeds with some individuals will be seen as reason enough to apply it to whole classes of people, whether they need it or not and even if other forms of treatment will better serve the same purpose. Third, even where the drug "works," it is a short-cut solution that deals with the problem without really solving it. The sex offender whose behavior is controlled in this way has not been cured of the psychological deformities that caused him to commit the offenses in the first place. In the presence of this poweful pill we would probably cease our attempts to find more fundamental but less drastic ways of helping him.

Finally, there are the irreversible biomedical interventions in which surgery or a drug permanently changes behavior. So far as I know, none of these interventions have yet emerged from the laboratory where the dogs, cats, and monkeys are the subjects, though we hear rumors of occasional experiments involving human subjects. Because of unpredictable side effects for most if not all of these biomedical interventions, the state of the art does not suggest as early a general application as our Delphi psychiatrist thought. Few judges will be willing to order psychosurgery that has an appreciable chance of failure, and fewer surgeons will be willing to carry it out, the laws on malpractice and medical assault being what they are.

Where the Meanest Citizen is Sovereign

But suppose that the state of the art advances to the level of certainty that we have with operations such as appendectomies? Could a judge in good conscience offer a convicted defendant a choice between amygdalectomy (with assurance of success of a very high probability) and a lifetime of prison? If we deny the judge the right to present this choice to the defendant, with all the safeguards of informed consent, is this not to deny the offender the right to a free life and to insist that to protect his interests we must lock him up for good? But if we do allow the judge to offer this choice, we do not confer on him more power than any judge should have? Not only can he order a lifetime of misery but he can make this order the alternative to submission to an intervention that will forever change the offender into something other than he is. This dilemma is coming. Its resolution touches the limits of power and its permitted use in a free society.

Over a century ago, John Stuart Mill wrote:

... the only purpose for which power can be rightfully exercised over any member of a civilized community, against his will, is to prevent harm to others. His own good, either physical or moral, is not a sufficient warrant. He cannot rightfully be compelled to do or forebear because it will be better for him to do so, because it will make him happier, because, in the opinions of others, to do so would be wise, or even right. These are good reasons for remonstrating with him, or reasoning with him, or persuading him, or entreating him, but not for compelling him, or visiting him with any evil in case he do otherwise. To justify that, the conduct from which it is desired to deter him must be calculated to produce evil to someone else. The only part of the conduct of anyone, for which he is amenable to society, is that which concerns others. In the part which merely concerns himself, his independence is, of right, absolute. Over himself, over his own body and mind, the individual is sovereign.[3]

That is a justly famous passage; it has come to be a part of the doctrine on which our civil liberties are based. We breach it at great peril to the liberties of every citizen, not merely to the liberties of the criminals who seem to deserve so little from us. When the state takes a man into custody, a defiant hero like Bonhoeffer or Solzhenitsyn may deny the state the custody of his will. Criminals are lesser men. They can indeed be compelled by threatening them with evil if they do otherwise. By taking them into custody we have protected others from the evil they might do. At the same time we have denied ourselves the right to do anything else to them, no matter how much good we think it may do them.

It is sometimes argued that we will do whatever technology enables us to do. This pronouncement of despair runs counter to the evidence of human experience. We have been able to muster enough repugnance for capital punishment to abolish it entirely in most civilized countries and to use it sparingly in our own, even though technology has given us extremely efficient and apparently painless ways of carrying it out. For millenia we have known that castration will eliminate libido and thereby incapacitate the sex offender, but this practice has been abandoned, even in Denmark where its rationalization was most plausible. All of us are safer when we set firm limits on what we allow the state to do to any of us. Once we allow unrestrained pragmatism to govern our decisions, even in the disposition of the unworthiest people, we generate an ethical cancer that will destroy the vitality of free institutions and the security of free people. Let us hope that when science offers criminal justice a foolproof drug or surgical procedure to stop criminal behavior, we will be principled enough to reject it.

Notes

1. Israel Goldiamond, "Toward a Constructional Approach to Social Problems," *Behaviorism* 2, no. 1 (Spring 1974): 1-82.

2. Comptroller General of the United States, *Behavior Modification Programs: The Bureau of Prisons' Alternative to Long Term Segregation* (Washington, D.C.: General Accounting Office, 5 August 1975).

3. John Stuart Mill, *On Liberty* (1859), in Edwin Burtt, (ed.), *The English Philosophers From Bacon to Mill* (New York: Random House, 1939), p. 956.

About the Authors

John P. Conrad, Senior Fellow, Center on Crime and Justice, is codirector of the Academy for Contemporary Problems' Dangerous Offender Project.

He received the bachelor's degree in political science from the University of California and the master's degree in social service administration from the University of Chicago. He has held teaching appointments at the University of California at Davis and the University of Pennsylvania, and is currently adjunct professor of sociology at The Ohio State University. He also served as a visiting expert at the United Nations Asia and Far East Institute for the Prevention of Crime and the Treatment of Offenders in Tokyo, Japan.

Before coming to the academy, Mr. Conrad was chief of the Center for Crime Prevention and Rehabilitation of the Law Enforcement Assistance Administration and a consultant to the National Advisory Commission on Criminal Justice Standards and Goals. A career criminologist who spent 20 years in the administration of the California Department of Corrections, Mr. Conrad's experience also includes work with the United States Bureau of Prisons, an appointment as a Senior Fulbright Fellow in criminology at the London School of Economics, and associate director of the International Survey of Corrections. In addition, he was a consultant to the President's Commission on Law Enforcement and the Administration of Justice. Mr. Conrad has written numerous papers and *Crime and Its Correction*, and was chief editor of the *Journal of Research in Crime and Delinquency* from 1974 to 1976.

Simon Dinitz, Senior Fellow, Center on Crime and Justice, is codirector of the Academy for Contemporary Problems' Dangerous Offender Project.

He received the bachelor's degree from Vanderbilt University and the master's and doctoral degrees from the University of Wisconsin.

Dr. Dinitz, is a professor of sociology and has been a member of The Ohio State University faculty since 1951. He has previously held a joint appointment at The Ohio State University as a research associate in psychiatry and was a visiting professor to the Universities of Tel Aviv, Wisconsin and Southern California.

Dr. Dinitz is the author or coauthor of ten books and numerous articles and reports, and he received the American Psychiatric Association's Hofheimer Prize in 1967 for *Schizophrenics in the Community: An Experiment in the Prevention of Hospitalization*. In addition, he received awards for outstanding teaching including the O.S.U. Alumni Award for Distinguished Teaching. In 1974 he received the Sutherland Award of the American Society of Criminology for outstanding contributions to that field.

Dr. Dinitz has been a member or trustee of numerous government and civic groups, including the United Nations Social Defense Research Institute, the

American Sociological Association Section on Criminology, the Ohio Governor's Task Force on Corrections, the Ohio Task Force on Mental Health and Retardation, and the International Advisory Board of the Institute of Criminology of the University of Tel Aviv. He is a former president of the American Society of Criminology and a former editor of its journal, *Criminology*.

Harold Goldman is a professor in the Department of Pharmacology, Wayne State University Medical School. Previously, he was a professor in the Department of Psychiatry at The Ohio State University and held an adjunct appointment in pharmacology. In addition to his laboratory research, Dr. Goldman has been involved for many years in studies of the biological substrates of sociopathy. This work is part of a more general concern with diseases of arousal.

Stephen J. Pfohl is assistant professor in sociology at Boston College. He received the B.A. from The Catholic University of America, the M.A. from The Ohio State University, and the Ph.D. from The Ohio State University in 1977. His recent publications have focused on the discovery of violence and the implications of right to treatment litigation. He is currently completing a monograph entitled *The Social Construction of Psychiatric Reality*, a study of the social interaction entailed in predicting dangerousness and mental illness for the criminally insane.

Stephan Van Dine is a research associate on the Dangerous Offender Project at the Academy for Contemporary Problems. Mr. Van Dine received the B.A. in Political Science from Wheaton College (Illinois) and the M.P.A. from the School of Public Administration at The Ohio State University. He has been involved in policy action research with the Ohio Adult Parole Authority, the Franklin County (Ohio) Sheriff's Department, and the Portland (Oregon) Police Department Planning and Research Department.